Integrated Chinese

Integrated Chinese

中文聽說讀寫

Traditional Character Edition

WORKBOOK

2nd Edition

Tao-chung Yao and Yuehua Liu

Yea-fen Chen, Liangyan Ge, Nyan-Ping Bi & Xiaojun Wang

CHENG & TSUI COMPANY ▲ BOSTON

Copyright © 2005, 1997 Tao-chung Yao, Yuehua Liu, Yea-fen Chen, Liangyan Ge, Nyan-Ping Bi and Xiaojun Wang

Second Edition

10 09 08 07 06   10 9 8 7 6 5 4 3 2

Published by
Cheng & Tsui Company, Inc.
25 West Street
Boston, MA 02111-1213 USA
Fax (617) 426-3669
www.cheng-tsui.com
"Bringing Asia to the World"™

Integrated Chinese Level 1 Part 1 Workbook
Traditional Character Edition
ISBN 0-88727-461-7
ISBN-13 978-0-88727-461-9

The *Integrated Chinese* series includes books, workbooks, character workbooks, audio products, multimedia products, teacher's resources, and more. Visit **www.cheng-tsui.com** for more information on the other components of *Integrated Chinese*.

Printed in the United States of America

THE INTEGRATED CHINESE SERIES

The *Integrated Chinese* series is a two-year course that includes textbooks, workbooks, character workbooks, audio CDs, CD-ROMs, DVDs and teacher's resources.

Textbooks introduce Chinese language and culture through a series of dialogues and narratives, with culture notes, language use and grammar explanations, and exercises.

Workbooks follow the format of the textbooks and contain a wide range of integrated activities that teach the four language skills of listening, speaking, reading and writing.

Character Workbooks help students learn Chinese characters in their correct stroke order. Special emphasis is placed on the radicals that are frequently used to compose Chinese characters.

Audio CDs include the narratives, dialogues and vocabulary presented in the textbooks, as well as pronunciation and listening exercises that correspond to the workbooks.

Teacher's Resources contain helpful guidance and additional activities online.

Multimedia CD-ROMs are divided into sections of listening, speaking, reading and writing, and feature a variety of supplemental interactive games and activities for students to test their skills and get instant feedback.

Workbook DVD shows listening comprehension dialogues from the Level 1 Part 1 Workbook, presented in contemporary settings in color video format.

PUBLISHER'S NOTE

When *Integrated Chinese* was first published in 1997, it set a new standard with its focus on the development and integration of the four language skills (listening, speaking, reading, and writing). Today, to further enrich the learning experience of the many users of *Integrated Chinese* worldwide, the Cheng & Tsui Company is pleased to offer the revised, updated and expanded second edition of *Integrated Chinese*. We would like to thank the many teachers and students who, by offering their valuable insights and suggestions, have helped *Integrated Chinese* evolve and keep pace with the many positive changes in the field of Chinese language instruction. *Integrated Chinese* continues to offer comprehensive language instruction, with many new features.

The Cheng & Tsui Asian Language Series is designed to publish and widely distribute quality language learning materials created by leading instructors from around the world. We welcome readers' comments and suggestions concerning the publications in this series. Please send feedback to our Editorial Department (e-mail: **editor@cheng-tsui.com**), or contact the following members of our Editorial Board.

CONTENTS

Introduction: Pronunciation Exercises   1

Lesson 1: Greetings   11

▼▼▼▼▼▼▼▼▼▼▼▼▼▼▼▼▼▼▼▼▼▼▼▼▼▼▼▼▼▼▼▼▼▼▼▼▼

▼ ▼

▼▼▼▼▼▼▼▼▼▼▼▼▼▼▼▼▼▼▼▼▼▼▼▼▼▼▼▼▼▼▼▼▼▼▼▼▼

PREFACE

In designing the Level One workbook exercises for *Integrated Chinese*, we strove to give equal emphasis to the students' listening, speaking, reading and writing skills. There are different difficulty levels in order to provide variety and flexibility to suit different curriculum needs. Teachers should assign the exercises at their discretion; they should not feel pressured into using all of them and should feel free to use them out of sequence, if appropriate. Moreover, teachers can complement this workbook with their own exercises.

The exercises in each lesson are divided into two parts. The exercises in Part One are for the first dialogue and those in Part Two are for the second dialogue. This way, the two dialogues in each lesson can be taught separately. The teacher can use the first two or three days to teach the first dialogue and ask the students to do all the exercises in Part One, then go on to teach the second dialogue. The teacher can also give the two separate vocabulary tests for the two dialogues so as to reduce the pressure of memorizing too many new words at the same time.

Listening Comprehension

All too often listening comprehension is sacrificed in a formal classroom setting because of time constraints. Students tend to focus their time and energy on the mastery of a few grammar points. This workbook tries to remedy this imbalance by including a substantial number of listening comprehension exercises. There are two categories of listening exercises; both can be done on the students' own time or in the classroom. In either case, it is important to have the instructor review the students' answers for accuracy.

The first category of listening exercises, which is at the beginning of this section, is based on the text of each lesson. For the exercises to be meaningful, students should *first* study the vocabulary list, and *then* listen to the recordings *before* attempting to read the texts. The questions are provided to help students' aural understanding of the texts and to test their reading comprehension.

The second category of listening exercises consists of an audio CD recording of two or more mini-dialogues or narratives. These exercises are designed to give students extra practice on the vocabulary and grammar points introduced in the lesson. Some of the exercises, especially ones that ask students to choose among several possible answers, are significantly more difficult than others. These exercises should be assigned towards the end of the lesson, when the students have become familiar with the content of the lesson.

Speaking Exercises

Here, too, there are two types of exercises. They are designed for different levels of proficiency within each lesson and should be assigned at the appropriate time.

To help students apply their newly-acquired vocabulary and grammatical understanding to meaningful communication, we first ask them questions related to the dialogues and narratives, and then ask them questions related to their own lives. These questions require a one- or two-sentence answer. By stringing together short questions and answers, students can construct their own mini-dialogues, practice in pairs or take turns asking or answering questions.

Once they have gained some confidence, students can progress to the more difficult questions, where they are invited to express opinions on a number of topics. Typically, these questions are abstract, so they gradually teach students to express their opinions in longer conversations. As the school year progresses, these types of questions should take up more class discussion time. Because this second type of speaking exercise is quite challenging, it should be attempted only *after* students are well grounded in the grammar and vocabulary of a particular lesson. Usually, this occurs *not immediately* after students have completed the first part of the speaking exercises.

Reading Comprehension

For the first seven lessons, the reading exercises appear in several different formats, including matching, translations, answering questions in English or answering multiple choice questions based on reading texts. There are also some authentic materials and modified authentic materials. Starting with Lesson 8, the format for reading exercises is fixed. The first section of the lesson asks questions based on the dialogues in the textbook. The second section offers several reading passages with questions that are relevant to the themes of the current lesson.

Writing and Grammar Exercises

Grammar and Usage

These drills and exercises are designed to solidify students' grasp of important grammar points. Through brief exchanges, students answer questions using specific grammatical forms, or are given sentences to complete. Because they must provide context for these exercises, students cannot treat them as simple mechanical repetition drills.

In the last three lessons, students are introduced to increasingly sophisticated and abstract vocabulary. Corresponding exercises help them to grasp the nuances of new words. For example, synonyms are a source of great difficulty, so exercises are provided to help students distinguish between them.

Translation

Translation has been a tool for language teaching throughout the ages, and positive student feedback confirms our belief that it continues to play an important role. The exercises we have devised serve to reinforce two primary areas: one, to get students to apply specific grammatical structures; and two, to allow students to build their ever-increasing vocabulary. Ultimately, our hope is that this dual-pronged approach will enable students to understand that it takes more than just literal translation to convey an idea in a foreign language.

Writing Practice

This is the culmination of the written exercises, and it is where students learn to express themselves in writing. Many of the topics overlap with those used in oral practice. We expect that students will find it easier to put in writing what they have already learned to express orally.

Introduction

Pronunciation Exercises

PART ONE

I. Single Words

Listen carefully and circle the correct answer.

A. Initials

1.	a. pà	b. bà
2.	a. pí	b. bí
3.	a. nán	b. mán
4.	a. fú	b. hú
5.	a. tīng	b. dīng
6.	a. tǒng	b. dǒng
7.	a. nán	b. lán
8.	a. niàn	b. liàn
9.	a. gàn	b. kàn
10.	a. kuì	b. huì
11.	a. kǎi	b. hǎi
12.	a. kuā	b. huā
13.	a. jiān	b. qiān
14.	a. yú	b. qú
15.	a. xiāng	b. shāng
16.	a. chú	b. rú
17.	a. zhá	b. zá
18.	a. zì	b. cì
19.	a. sè	b. shè
20.	a. sè	b. cè
21.	a. zhǒng	b. jiǒng
22.	a. shēn	b. sēn
23.	a. rù	b. lù

B. Finals

	a.	b.
1.	tuō	tōu
2.	guǒ	gǒu
3.	duò	dòu
4.	diū	dōu
5.	liú	lóu
6.	yǒu	yǔ
7.	nǚ	nǚ
8.	lú	lǘ
9.	yuán	yán
10.	píng	pín
11.	làn	luàn
12.	huán	hán
13.	fèng	fèn
14.	bèng	bèn
15.	lún	léng
16.	bīn	bīng
17.	kěn	kǔn
18.	héng	hóng
19.	téng	tóng
20.	kēng	kōng
21.	pàn	pàng
22.	fǎn	fǎng
23.	dǎn	dǎng
24.	mín	míng
25.	pēn	pān
26.	rén	rán
27.	mán	mén

C. Tones: First and Fourth (Level and Falling)

	a.	b.
1.	pō	pò
2.	pān	pàn
3.	wù	wū

4.a. tà   b. tā

5.a. qū   b. qù

6.a. sì   b. sī

7.a. fēi   b. fèi

8.a. duì   b. duī

9.a. xià   b. xiā

10.a. yā   b. yà

D. Tones: Second and Third (Rising and Low)

1.a. mǎi   b. mái

2.a. fǎng   b. fáng

3.a. dá   b. dǎ

4.a. tú   b. tǔ

5.a. nǐ   b. ní

6.a. wú   b. wǔ

7.a. bǎ   b. bá

8.a. shí   b. shǐ

9.a. huǐ   b. huí

10.a. féi   b. fěi

11.a. mǎ   b. má

12.a. dí   b. dǐ

13.a. láo   b. lǎo

14.a. gé   b. gě

15.a. zhǐ   b. zhí

E. Tones: All Four Tones   5 - 06   X

1.a. bà b   b. bā

2.a. pí b   b. pì

3.a. méi a   b. měi

4.a. wēn a   b. wěn

5.a. zǎo b   b. zāo

6.a. yōu a   b. yóu   say you

7.a. guāng b   b. guǎng

8.a. zhuāng a   b. zhuàng

9.a. qì   *a*   b. qí   —

10.a. mào *b*   b. máo

11.a. bǔ   *b*   b. bù

12.a. kuàng *b*   b. kuāng

13.a. jú   *a*   b. jǔ

14.a. qiáng *b*   b. qiāng   —

15.a. xián *a*   b. xiān

16.a. yǒng *b*   b. yòng

17.a. zú   *a*   b. zū

18.a. cí *ti b*   b. cǐ

19.a. suī *a*   b. suí   —

20.a. zhèng *a*   b. zhēng

21.a. chòu *b*   b. chóu   — *cho*

22.a. shuāi *b*   b. shuài

23.a. wǒ   *a*   b. wò   *wall*

24.a. yào *b*   b. yáo   —

25.a. huī *b*   b. huì   *gui* — —

26.a. rú   *a*   b. rù   —

27.a. rén *a*   b. rèn   —

F. Comprehensive Exercise

1.a. jiā | (b.) zhā   *b*   ✳

(2.a.) chuí *2*   b. qué   *a*

3.a. chǎng *3* | *a*   b. qiǎng *a*

4.a. xū *2*   b. shū   *b*

5.a. shuǐ *b* | *b*   b. xuě   —

6.a. zǎo *b* | *b*   b. zhǎo   —

7.a. zǎo *a* | *b*   b. cǎo

8.a. sōu *a* | *a*   b. shōu

9.a. tōu *a* | *b*   b. tuō

10.a. dǒu *à* | *b*   b. duō

11.a. duǒ *a* | *b*   b. zuǒ

12.a. mǎi *b* | *a*   b. měi

▼▼▼▼▼▼▼▼▼▼▼▼▼▼▼▼▼▼▼▼▼▼▼▼▼▼▼▼▼▼▼▼▼▼▼▼▼▼▼

13.a. shào   (b.) xiào   *a*

14.a. chóu   (b.) qiú   *b*

(15.) a. yuè   b. yè   *b*

16.a. jiǔ   b. zhǒu   *b*

17.a. nǔ   b. nǚ   *b*

18.a. zhú   *a*   b. jú   *a*

19.a. jì   *a*   b. zì   *a*

20.a. liè   (b.) lüè   *b*

21.(a.) jīn   b. zhēn   *a*

22.a. xiǔ   b. shǒu   *a*

23.a. kǔn   (b.) hěn   *b*

24.(a.) shǎo   b. xiǎo   *b*

25.a. zhǎng   (b.) jiǎng   *b*

26.a. qū   (b.) chū   *a*

II. Tone Combination Exercise

You will hear one word at a time. Write down the tones in the blank. Use 1-4 for the four tones, and 5 for neutral tones.

Example: If you hear the word "Zhōngwén," you will write "1, 2" in the blank.

A.

1. 1, 3   *1, 4*
2. 1, 5   *2, 5*
3. 2, ∨   *4, 2*
4. 3 2   *3, 1*
5. 1, 2   *1, 1*
6. 2, 3   *4, 3*
7. 1, 2   *2, 4*
8. 2, 3   *1, 3*
9. 1, 4   *1, 5*
10. 1, 3   *4, 4*

11. 1, 3   *4, 5*
12. 2, 5   *1, 2*
13. 2, 4   *1, 2*
14. 1, 5   *2, 2*
15. 2, ∨   *1, 4*
16. 1, 2   *4, 1*
17. 1, 5   *3, 5*
18. 2, 5   *1, 5*
19. 1, 4   *3, 4*
20. 1, 3   *2, 3*

21. 1, ∨   *1, 2*
22. 1, 2   *2, 1*
23. 1, 5   *4, 5*
24. 2, ∨   *3, 2*
25. 1, 2   *2, 1*
26. 2, 3   *1, 4*
27. 1, 3   *3, 1*
28. 1 4 2   *1, 32*
29. 1 2 4   *1, 1, 1*
30. 1 2 4   *2, 4, 4*

B.

1._____	10._____	19._____	28._____
2._____	11._____	20._____	29._____
3._____	12._____	21._____	30._____
4._____	13._____	22._____	
5._____	14._____	23._____	
6._____	15._____	24._____	
7._____	16._____	25._____	
8._____	17._____	26._____	
9._____	18._____	27._____	

PART TWO

I. Initials and Simple Finals

Fill in the blanks with appropriate initials or simple finals.

A.1. __a	A.2. p__	A.3. __u	A.4. l__
B.1. f__	B.2. n__	B.3. __i	B.4. __u
C.1. __a	C.2. l__	C.3. l__	C.4. __u
D.1. __u	D.2. t__	D.3. n__	D.4. n__
E.1. __e	E.2. __u	E.3. __a	
F.1. g__	F.2. k__	F.3. h__	
G.1. __u	G.2. __i	G.3. __u	
H.1. j__	H.2. q__	H.3. x__	
I.1. __a	I.2. __e	I.3. __i	I.4. __u
J.1. __u	J.2. c__	J.3. __u	J.4. __i
K.1. __i	K.2. s__	K.3. __a	K.4. q__
L.1. __a	L.2. __i	L.3. s__	L.4. __u
M.1. c__	M.2. __i	M.3. __u	M.4. __a
N.1. __u	N.2. r__	N.3. ch__	N.4. __e

II. Tones

Listen to the CD and mark the correct tone marks.

A.1. he	A.2. ma	A.3. pa	A.4. di
B.1. nü	B.2. re	B.3. chi	B.4. zhu
C.1. mo	C.2. qu	C.3. ca	C.4. si
D.1. tu	D.2. fo	D.3. ze	D.4. ju

▼▼

E.1. lü	E.2. bu	E.3. xi	E.4. shi
F.1. gu	F.2. se	F.3. ci	F.4. ku
G.1. mang	G.2. quan	G.3. yuan	G.4. yue
H.1. yi	H.2. er	H.3. san	H.4. si
I.1. ba	I.2. qi	I.3. liu	I.4. wu
J.1. jiu	J.2. shi	J.3. tian	J.4. jin
K.1. mu	K.2. shui	K.3. huo	K.4. ren
L.1. yu	L.2. zhuang	L.3. qun	L.4. zhong

III. Compound Finals

A. Fill in the blanks with compound finals.

1.a. zh____	1.b. t____	1.c. k____	1.d. j____
2.a. x____	2.b. q____	2.c. j____	2.d. d____
3.a. x____	3.b. zh____	3.c. t____	3.d. g____
4.a. sh____	4.b. b____	4.c. z____	4.d. q____
5.a. j____	5.b. d____	5.c. x____	5.d. ch____
6.a. zh____	6.b. l____	6.c. k____	6.d. j____
7.a. s____	7.b. x____	7.c. p____	7.d. ch____

B. Fill in the blanks with compound finals and mark appropriate tone marks.

1.a. m____	1.b. zh____	1.c. sh____	1.d. zh____
2.a sh____	2.b. t____	2.c. l____	2.d. b____
3.a. s____	3.b. j____	3.c. k____	3.d. d____
4.a. l____	4.b. q____	4.c. t____	4.d. x____
5.a. f____	5.b. p____	5.c. x____	5.d. j____
6.a. b____	6.b. j____	6.c. q____	6.d. t____
7.a. l____	7.b. g____	7.c. q____	7.d. x____

IV. Neutral Tones

Listen to the CD and mark the tone marks.

A.1. guanxi	A.2. kuzi	A.3. shifu	A.4. keqi
B.1. zhuozi	B.2. gaosu	B.3. shufu	B.4. women
C.1. gege	C.2. weizi	C.3. dongxi	C.4. yisi
D.1. nimen	D.2. shihou	D.3. chuqu	D.4. pengyou
E.1. meimei	E.2. xihuan	E.3. jiaozi	E.4. xiansheng
F.1. zenme	F.2. didi	F.3. erzi	F.4. xiexie
G.1. jiejie	G.2. mafan	G.3. bobo	G.4. yizi

V. Exercises for Initials, Finals, and Tones: Monosyllabic Words

Transcribe what you hear into pinyin with tone marks.

A.1._____	A.2. _____	A.3._____	A.4._____
B.1._____	B.2._____	B.3._____	B.4._____
C.1._____	C.2._____	C.3._____	C.4._____
D.1._____	D.2._____	D.3._____	D.4._____
E.1._____	E.2._____	E.3._____	E.4._____
F.1._____	F.2._____	F.3._____	F.4._____
G.1._____	G.2._____	G.3._____	G.4._____
H.1._____	H.2._____	H.3._____	H.4._____
I.1._____	I.2._____	I.3._____	I.4._____

VI. Exercises for Initials, Finals, and Tones: Bisyllabic Words

Put the letter corresponding to the word you hear into the parentheses.

( )   A.1.   a. làoshī   b. lǎoshī   c. lǎoshí
( )   A.2.   a. Méiguó   b. Měiguó   c. Mèiguó
( )   A.3.   a. zhàopiàn   b. zhāopiàn   c. zháopiàn
( )   A.4.   a. wànfàn   b. wǎnfān   c. wǎnfàn
( )   B.1.   a. shēngrì   b. shéngrì   c. shěngrì
( )   B.2.   a. zāijiàn   b. zàijiàn   c. záijiàn
( )   B.3.   a. xuéshēng   b. xuèsheng   c. xuésheng
( )   B.4.   a. diànyǐng   b. diānyǐng   c. diànyìng
( )   C.1.   a. zuòtiān   b. zuótiān   c. zuótiàn
( )   C.2.   a. suírán   b. suírán   c. suīràn
( )   C.3.   a. xièxiè   b. shèshe   c. xièxie
( )   C.4.   a. kāfēi   b. káfēi   c. kāifēi
( )   D.1.   a. kēlè   b. kělè   c. kělà
( )   D.2.   a. píngcháng   b. pēngchán   c. píngchèng
( )   D.3.   a. gōngzuò   b. gōngzhuò   c. gōngzòu
( )   D.4.   a. piàoliàng   b. piāoliang   c. piàoliang
( )   E.1.   a. fángbiàn   b. fāngbián   c. fāngbiàn
( )   E.2.   a. wèntì   b. wèntí   c. wěntí
( )   E.3.   a. fùxí   b. fùxi   c. fǔxí
( )   E.4.   a. rōngyì   b. lóngyì   c. róngyì

▼▼

( ) F.1. a. kāishǐ   b. kāixǐ   c. kāisǐ

( ) F.2. a. loùdiǎn   b. liùdiǎn   c. liùdǎn

( ) F.3. a. píjiǔ   b. pìjiǔ   c. peíjiǔ

( ) F.4. a. nǚ'ér   b. nǚ'èr   c. nǚ'ér

VII. Exercises for Initials, Finals, and Tones: Cities

Read the following words and identify which cities they are. Put the letter corresponding to the city name into the parentheses.

Example: Mài'āmì   ☐   <u>Miami</u>

( )   1. Bōshìdùn   a. Venice

( )   2. Lúndūn   b. Toronto

( )   3. Niǔyuē   c. Boston

( )   4. Bālí   d. Chicago

( )   5. Zhījiāgē   e. Seattle

( )   6. Běijīng   f. New York

( )   7. Luòshānjī   g. Paris

( )   8. Duōlúnduō   h. London

( )   9. Xīyǎtú   i. Beijing

( )   10. Wēinísī   j. Los Angeles

VIII. Exercises for Initials, Finals, and Tones: Celebrities

Read the following words and write each celebrity's name in English.

1. Mǎdānnà   _____

2. Màikè Jiékèsēn _____

3. Yīlìshābái Tàilè _____

4. Bābālā Sīcuìshān _____

5. Aòdàilì Hèběn   _____

6. Suǒfēiyǎ Luólán _____

7. Mǎlìlián Mènglù _____

IX. Exercises for Initials, Finals, and Tones: Countries

Transcribe what you hear into pinyin with tone marks and write each country name in English.

Example: <u>Rìběn</u> → <u>Japan</u>

1._____ → _____
2._____ → _____
3._____ → _____
4._____ → _____
5._____ → _____
6._____ → _____
7._____ → _____
8._____ → _____
9._____ → _____
10._____ → _____

X. Exercises for Initials, Finals, and Tones: American Presidents

Transcribe what you hear into pinyin with tone marks and write down each president's name in English.

1._____ → _____
2._____ → _____
3._____ → _____
4._____ → _____
5._____ → _____
6._____ → _____
7._____ → _____
8._____ → _____
9._____ → _____
10._____ → _____

LESSON 1 ▲ Greetings
第一課 ▲ 問好
Dì yí kè ▲ *Wèn hǎo*

Part One

DIALOGUE I: EXCHANGING GREETINGS

I. Listening Comprehension

A. Textbook Dialogue I (Multiple Choice)

(　) 1. What was the first thing that the man said to the woman?

    a. What's your name?　　b. I'm Mr. Wang.

    c. Are you Miss Li?　　d. How do you do!

(　) 2. What is the woman's full name?

    a. Wang Peng　　b. Li You

    c. Xing Li　　d. Jiao Li You

(　) 3. What is the man's full name?

    a. Wang Peng　　b. Li You

    c. Xing Wang　　d. Jiao Wang Peng

B. Workbook Dialogue I (Multiple Choice)

(　) These two people are:

    a. saying good-bye to each other.

    b. asking each other's name.

    c. greeting each other.

    d. asking each other's nationality.

C. Workbook Dialogue II (Multiple Choice)

(　) 1. The two speakers are most likely:

    a. brother and sister.

    b. father and daughter.

    c. old friends reuniting.

    d. strangers getting acquainted.

(   ) 2. Who are these two people?

    a. Mr. Li and Miss You

    b. Mr. Li and Miss Li

    c. Mr. Wang and Miss You

    d. Mr. Wang and Miss Wang

II. SPEAKING EXERCISES

A. Answer the questions in Chinese based on Textbook Dialogue I.

    1. How does Mr. Wang greet Miss Li in Chinese?

    2. What is Miss Li's reply?

    3. How does Mr. Wang ask what Miss Li's surname is?

    4. What is Mr. Wang's given name?

    5. How does Mr. Wang ask what Miss Li's given name is?

    6. What is Miss Li's given name?

B. You meet a Chinese student on campus:

    1. Greet him/her in Chinese.

    2. Ask his/her name.

▼▼▼

III. READING COMPREHENSION

Read the passage and answer the questions. (True/False)

你好，先生。請問您貴姓？

Questions:

( ) 1. The question is addressed to a man.

( ) 2. The speaker is talking to his/her friend.

( ) 3. The sentence occurs at the end of a conversation.

( ) 4. We do not know the addressee's family name.

IV. WRITING & GRAMMAR EXERCISES

Grammar and Usage

A. Give the Chinese characters for the following sentences in pinyin.

1. Nín guì xìng?

2. Nǐ jiào shénme míngzi?

B. Rearrange the given Chinese words into a sentence, using the English sentence as a clue.

叫 / 名字 / 你 / 請問 / 什麼

(May I ask what your name is?)

C. Answer the following questions in Chinese.

1. 您貴姓？

2. 你叫什麼名字？

Translation

Translate the following sentences, making use of the Chinese words or phrases in parentheses.

1. May I ask what your surname is? (請問, 貴姓)

2. My surname is Li. My name is Li You. (我姓..., 我叫...)

Writing Practice

Write your Chinese name, if you have one, in characters.

▼▼

Part Two

DIALOGUE II: ASKING ONE'S STATUS

I. Listening Comprehension

A. Textbook Dialogue II (True/False)

Quote the key sentence from the dialogue to support your answer.

     ( ) 1. Miss Li is a student.

     ( ) 2. Mr. Wang is a teacher.

     ( ) 3. Mr. Wang is an American.

     ( ) 4. Miss Li is a Chinese.

B. Workbook Dialogue III (Multiple Choice)

     ( ) Which of the following is true?

         a. Both the man and the woman are Chinese.

         b. Both the man and the woman are American.

         c. The man is Chinese and the woman is American.

         d. The man is American and the woman is Chinese.

C. Workbook Dialogue IV (Multiple Choice)

     ( ) Which of the following is true?

         a. Both the man and the woman are teachers.

         b. Both the man and the woman are students.

         c. The man is a teacher. The woman is a student.

         d. The man is a student. The woman is a teacher.

II. Speaking Exercises

A. Answer the questions in Chinese based on Textbook Dialogue II.

     1. How does Miss Li ask whether Mr. Wang is a teacher or not?

     2. Is Mr. Wang a teacher?

     3. Is Miss Li a teacher?

     4. What is Mr. Wang's nationality?

     5. What is Miss Li's nationality?

B. *You meet a middle-aged Chinese person on campus. Try to ask politely in Chinese whether he/she is a teacher.*

C. *Introduce yourself in Chinese to a Chinese student. Tell him/her what your name is and whether you are a student.*

D. *You just met a foreign student who can speak Chinese.*

     1. Ask him/her whether he/she is Chinese.

     2. Tell him/her that you are American.

III. Reading Comprehension

A. *Read the passage and answer the questions. (True/False)*

王小姐是中國學生。李先生是美國老師。

Questions:

( ) 1. 王小姐姓王。

( ) 2. 王小姐是美國人。

( ) 3. 王小姐不是老師。

( ) 4. 李先生不是中國人。

( ) 5. 李先生是老師。

B. *Match the utterances on the left column with the appropriate responses on the right column. Write down the letter in the parentheses.*

( ) 1. 你好！   A. 是,我是老師。

( ) 2. 您貴姓？   B. 不,我是中國人。

( ) 3. 你是美國人嗎？   C. 我也是學生。

( ) 4. 你是老師嗎？   D. 我姓李。

( ) 5. 我是學生，你呢？   E. 你好！

C. *Based on your understanding of the passage below, fill out of the following form in English. Then answer the questions below.*

> 王先生叫王中師。王中師是美國人，不是中國人。王中師是學生，不是老師。李小姐叫李美生。李美生是中國老師，不是美國學生。

	Gender	Given name	Nationality	Occupation
王先生				
李小姐				

Questions (Multiple Choice):

(   ) 1. If you were the man's close friend, most often you would address him as:

     a. Wang Xiansheng.

     b. Xiansheng Wang.

     c. Wang.

     d. Zhongshi.

(   ) 2. If you were being introduced to the woman for the first time, it would be most appropriate for you to address her as:

     a. Li Xiaojie.

     b. Xiaojie Li.

     c. Li Meisheng.

     d. Meisheng.

▼▼▼▼▼▼▼▼▼▼▼▼▼▼▼▼▼▼▼▼▼▼▼▼▼▼▼▼▼▼▼▼▼▼▼▼▼▼▼

D. Chinese Business Cards

Below are four Chinese business cards. Circle all of the characters that you recognize, and underline the characters denoting family names.

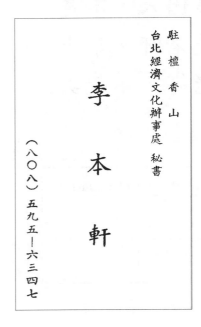

IV. Writing & Grammar Exercises

Grammar and Usage

A. Give the Chinese characters for the following sentences in pinyin.

　　1. Qǐng wèn, nǐ shì xuésheng ma?

　　2. Wǒ shì Zhōngguórén. Nǐ ne?

3. Wǒ bú xìng Wáng, wǒ xìng Lǐ.

4. Nín shì lǎoshī, wǒ shì xuésheng.

5. Nǐ shì Měiguórén, wǒ yě shì Měiguórén.

B. *Rearrange the given Chinese words into a sentence, using the English sentence as a clue.*

1. 姓 / 王 / 嗎 / 你
(Is your surname Wang?)

2. 嗎 / 是 / 你 / 學生 / 美國
(Are you an American student?)

3. 中國 / 是 / 人 / 我 / 不
(I am not Chinese.)

4. 小姐 / 先生 / 美國人 / 美國人 / 王 / 李 /
也 / 是 / 是
(Miss Li is American. Mr. Wang is also American.)

C. *Answer the following questions in Chinese.*

1. 你是學生嗎？

2. 李小姐是美國人。你呢？

3. 王先生是中國學生。你呢？

D. *Form the questions that would elicit the following statements.*

   Example: 我是學生。→ 你是學生嗎？

   1. 我是美國人。

   2. 我姓李。

   3. 王老師是中國人。

   4. 李小姐不是學生。

   5. 我也是學生。

E. *In each group, use* 也 *to connect the two sentences into a compound sentence.*

   Example: 李友是學生。/王朋是學生。
   → 李友是學生，王朋也是學生。

▼▼▼▼▼▼▼▼▼▼▼▼▼▼▼▼▼▼▼▼▼▼▼▼▼▼▼▼▼▼▼▼▼▼▼▼▼▼▼

1. 你是美國人。/我是美國人。

2. 李小姐不是中國人。/李先生不是中國人。

3. 你不姓王。/我不姓王。

4. 王先生是老師。/李小姐是老師。

Translation

Translate the following sentences into Chinese, using the words or phrases in parentheses.

1. I am American. (是)

2. Are you Chinese? (是, 嗎)

3. I am a teacher. How about you? (呢)

4. *A:* I am an American student. Are you an American student, too? (也)

　B: No, I am a Chinese student. (不)

   5. Mr. Wang is not Chinese. Nor am I. (也不)

[Note: The following sentences contain supplementary vocabulary.]

   6. May I ask if you are Japanese?

   7. Mr. Wang is English. Mrs. Wang is Chinese.

   8. Mr. Li is not French. Mrs. Li is not French, either.

Writing Practice

Without looking at the book, write as many characters as you can from Lesson 1.

LESSON 2 ▲ Family
第二課 ▲ 家庭
Dì èr kè ▲ *Jiātíng*

Part One

DIALOGUE I: LOOKING AT A FAMILY PHOTO

I. Listening Comprehension

A. Textbook Dialogue I (True/False)

Quote the key sentence from the dialogue to support your answer.

( ) 1. The picture in question belongs to Wang Peng.

( ) 2. Little Gao doesn't have any younger brothers.

( ) 3. Little Gao's parents are in the picture.

( ) 4. All the people in the picture are members of Little Gao's family.

( ) 5. Mr. Li does not have any sons.

B. Workbook Dialogue I (Multiple Choice)

( ) Who are the people in the picture?

  a. The woman's father and mother.

  b. The woman's mother and younger sister.

  c. The woman's older sister and younger sister.

  d. The woman's mother and older sister.

II. Speaking Exercises

A. Answer the questions in Chinese based on Textbook Dialogue I.

1. Whose photo is on the wall?

2. How many people are there in Little Gao's family? Who are they?

3. Is the boy in the picture Little Gao's younger brother? How do you know?

4. Is the girl in the picture Little Gao's younger sister? How do you know?

B. Find a picture of your parents and use it to introduce your parents to your friends.

III. Reading Comprehension

A. Match the questions on the left with the appropriate replies on the right. Write down the letter in the parentheses.

(　)1. 這個人是誰？　　　　A. 是我的。

(　)2. 這張照片是誰的？　　B. 這是我爸爸。

(　)3. 你妹妹是學生嗎？　　C. 他有兒子，沒有 女兒。

(　)4. 李先生有女兒嗎？　　D. 我沒有弟弟。

(　)5. 你有弟弟嗎？　　　　E. 她是學生。

B. Read the following dialogue and answer the questions.

(Li You is nearsighted.)

王朋：李友，這張照片是你的嗎？

李友：是。這是我爸爸，這是我媽媽。

王朋：這個女孩子是誰？

李友：是我. . . (looking at the picture again more carefully)
　　　不是，不是，這不是我。

王朋：她是你妹妹嗎？

李友：也不是。她是高小姐。這是高小姐
　　　的照片，不是我的。

Questions (Multiple Choice):

(　) 1. Which of the following is correct?

　　a. Li You was looking at someone else's photo but mistook it for her own.

b. Li You was looking at her own photo but mistook it for someone else's.

c. Li You was looking at her sister's photo but mistook it for her own.

d. Li You was looking at her own photo but mistook it for her sister's.

(   ) 2. The girl in the picture turns out to be:

a. Li You's younger sister.   b. Wang Peng's younger sister.

c. Miss Gao.   d. Li You's older sister.

(   ) 3. Miss Gao must be someone:

a. Li You knows.

b. Wang Peng knows.

c. Li You and Wang Peng both know.

d. neither Li You nor Wang Peng know.

IV. Writing & Grammar Exercises

Grammar and Usage

A. Fill in the blanks with "這" *or* "那" *based on the descriptions for each situation.*

1. You point to a person standing about thirty feet away, and say:

＿＿＿＿個人是我的老師，他是中國人。

2. You hold a family photo in your hand, and say:

＿＿＿＿是我爸爸，＿＿＿＿是我媽媽。

3. You look down the hallway and recognize someone, and say:

＿＿＿＿個人叫李生一，是李友的爸爸。

4. You introduce to your friend a girl sitting at the same table, and say:

＿＿＿＿是李先生的女兒。

Translation

Translate the following sentences into Chinese, using the words or phrases in parentheses.

1. Little Wang, is this photograph yours? (是…嗎？)

2. Mr. Wang has no sons.

3. Is this person your mother?

4. Is this boy your younger brother?

5. *A:* Who is this person? (誰)

   B: She's my younger sister. (是)

6. *A:* Do you have any younger brothers? (有)

   B: No, I don't have any younger brothers. (沒有)

Writing Practice

Without looking at the textbook, write as many characters as you can from Lesson 2, Dialogue I.

Part Two

DIALOGUE II: ASKING ABOUT SOMEONE'S FAMILY

I. Listening Comprehension

A. Textbook Dialogue II (Multiple Choice)

(   ) 1. How many people are there in Little Zhang's family?

    a. 3   b. 4   c. 5   d. 6

(   ) 2. How many people are there in Li You's family?

    a. 3   b. 4   c. 5   d. 6

(   ) 3. How many older sisters does Little Zhang have?

    a. 0   b. 1   c. 2   d. 3

(   ) 4. How many younger sisters does Li You have?

    a. 0   b. 1   c. 2   d. 3

(   ) 5. How many older brothers does Little Zhang have?

    a. 0   b. 1   c. 2   d. 3

(   ) 6. How many younger brothers does Little Zhang have?

    a. 0   b. 1   c. 2   d. 3

(   ) 7. How many children do Little Zhang's parents have?

    a. 2   b. 3   c. 4   d. 5

(   ) 8. How many sons do Li You's parents have?

    a. 0   b. 1   c. 2   d. 3

(   ) 9. Little Zhang's father is a:

    a. lawyer.   b. teacher.   c. doctor.   d. student.

(   ) 10. Li You's mother is a:

    a. lawyer.   b. teacher.   c. doctor.   d. student.

B. Workbook Dialogue II (Multiple Choice)

(   ) 1. Which of the following is true?

    a. Both the man and the woman have older brothers.

    b. Both the man and the woman have younger brothers.

c. The man has an older brother but no younger brothers.

d. The man has a younger brother but no older brothers.

( ) 2. Why does the woman laugh at the end of the conversation? Because she finds it funny that:

a. neither the man nor she herself has any younger brothers.

b. neither the man nor she herself has any older brothers.

c. the man failed to count himself as his older brother's younger brother.

d. the man failed to count himself as his younger brother's older brother.

C. Workbook Dialogue III (Multiple Choice)

( ) 1. The man's mother is a:

a. teacher.   b. student.   c. doctor.   d. lawyer.

( ) 2. The woman's father is a:

a. teacher.   b. student.   c. doctor.   d. lawyer.

D. Workbook Dialogue IV (Multiple Choice)

( ) 1. How many brothers does the woman have?
a. 1   b. 2   c. 3   d. 4

( ) 2. How many daughters do the woman's parents have?
a. 1   b. 2   c. 3   d. 4

( ) 3. How many people in the woman's family are older than herself?
a. 2   b. 3   c. 4   d. 5

( ) 4. How many people in the man's family are younger than himself?
a. 0   b. 1   c. 2   d. 3

( ) 5. Why do the speakers disagree on the number of people in the man's family? Because he forgot to include:

a. his older brother.   b. his younger sister.

c. his younger brother.   d. himself.

▼▼

II. Speaking Exercises

A. Answer the questions in Chinese based on Textbook Dialogue II.

　　1. How many people are there in Little Zhang's family?

　　2. How many children do Little Zhang's parents have?

　　3. What is the birth order of Little Zhang?

　　4. How many brothers and sisters does Li You have?

　　5. What is the occupation of Little Zhang's father?

　　6. What is the occupation of Little Zhang's mother and Li You's mother?

　　7. How many people are there in Li You's family?

　　8. How many daughters do Li You's parents have?

B. Find a family picture and use it to introduce your family members to your friends.

C. Show your family photo to your partner and ask questions about each other's photo, such as who the person is, whether your partner has any brothers or sisters, what each of his/her family members does.

D. Following are four members of Wang You's family. Introduce them. Make sure that you mention what they do.

　　1. Wang You's older brother

　　2. Wang You's mother

　　3. Wang You's father

　　4. Wang You's younger brother

III. Reading Comprehension

A. This is a family portrait of the Gao family. Look at the photo carefully and identify each person.

1. 爸爸（ ）   2. 媽媽（ ）

3. 妹妹（ ）   4. 弟弟（ ）

B. *Match each Chinese word with its English equivalent by placing the letter in the appropriate parentheses.*

（ ）1. 爸爸   A. mother

（ ）2. 哥哥   B. younger sister

（ ）3. 弟弟   C. older sister

（ ）4. 妹妹   D. older brother

（ ）5. 媽媽   E. younger brother

（ ）6. 姐姐   F. father

（ ）7. 誰   G. how many

（ ）8. 幾   H. who

（ ）9. 誰的   I. whose

C. *Read the passage and answer the questions. (True/False)*

小高家有五個人，爸爸、媽媽、一個姐姐、一個妹妹和他。他的爸爸是醫生，媽媽是律師，姐姐是老師，他和妹妹都是學生。

Questions:

（ ）1. Little Gao has two sisters.

（ ）2. Little Gao has one brother.

（ ）3. Little Gao is the youngest child in his family.

（ ）4. Little Gao's parents have three children.

（ ）5. Little Gao's parents are both doctors.

（ ）6. Little Gao's sisters are both teachers.

（ ）7. Little Gao is a student.

▼▼▼▼▼▼▼▼▼▼▼▼▼▼▼▼▼▼▼▼▼▼▼▼▼▼▼▼▼▼▼▼▼▼▼▼▼▼

D. Read the passage and answer the questions. (True/False)

小王家有六個人。她的爸爸是老師，媽媽
是醫生。她有一個哥哥、兩個妹妹。她的
哥哥也是醫生，她和兩個妹妹都是學生。

Questions:

（　）1. Little Wang is the oldest child in the family.

（　）2. Little Wang's father and her brother are both teachers.

（　）3. Little Wang's parents have only one son.

（　）4. Little Wang's mother and brother are both doctors.

（　）5. All the girls in the Wang family are students.

E. Based on your understanding of the passage below, fill out of the following form in English. Then answer the questions below. (True/False)

小王：請問，你爸爸是律師嗎？

小高：不，他是老師。我家有兩個老師，
　　　三個醫生。

小王：你家有五個人嗎？

小高：不，我家有四個人。我和我媽媽都
　　　是醫生。我哥哥是老師，也是醫生。

Mark the proper spaces in the following form to indicate the profession of each member of Xiao Gao's family:

	Xiao Gao	Father	Mother	Brother
Lawyer				
Doctor				
Teacher				

▼ ▼

Questions:

( ) 1. Xiao Wang seems to know Xiao Gao's family very well.

( ) 2. Xiao Gao seems to have miscounted the people in his family.

( ) 3. Xiao Gao's older brother is not only a teacher, but also a doctor.

IV. Writing & Grammar Exercises

Grammar and Usage

A. Answer the following questions about your siblings in complete sentences, using 有 *or* 沒有 *. If the answer is positive, state how many there are.*

Examples: 1.A: 你有哥哥嗎？　　B: 我沒有哥哥。

2.A: 你有哥哥嗎？　　B: 我有三個哥哥。

1.A: 你有姐姐嗎？

B: ＿＿＿＿＿＿＿＿＿＿ 。

2.A: 你有妹妹嗎？

B: ＿＿＿＿＿＿＿＿＿＿ 。

3.A: 你有弟弟嗎？

B: ＿＿＿＿＿＿＿＿＿＿ 。

4.A: 你有哥哥嗎？

B: ＿＿＿＿＿＿＿＿＿＿ 。

B. Rewrite the following sentences using 都 *.*

Example: 小高是學生，王朋也是學生。

→ 小高、王朋都是學生。

1. 小高有姐姐，小張也有姐姐。

2. 王朋是學生，李友也是學生。

3. 這張照片是你的，那張照片也是你的。

4. 這個人姓李，那個人也姓李。

5. 李友沒有我的照片，王朋也沒有我的照片。

6. 他哥哥不是律師，他弟弟也不是律師。

7. 王朋有哥哥，小高有哥哥，李友有哥哥。

8. 我爸爸是醫生，我媽媽是醫生，我哥哥是律師。

C. *Fill in the blanks with the appropriate question words.* (什麼、誰、誰的、幾)

1. A: _____名字叫王朋？   B: 他的名字叫王朋。

2. A: 李老師家有_____個人？   B: 他家有三個人。

3. A: 你爸爸是做_____的？   B: 我爸爸是醫生。

4. A: 你妹妹叫_____名字？   B: 我妹妹叫高美美。

5. A: 那個美國人是_____？   B: 他叫 David Smith, 是我的老師。

6. A: 你有 _____ 張你媽媽的   B: 我有兩張。
照片？

Translation

Translate the following sentences into Chinese, using the words or phrases in parentheses.

1. Mr. Zhang has three daughters.

2. A: Is he your older brother?

   B: No, he's my father. (不是)

3. A: How many older sisters do you have? (有, 幾)

   B: I have two older sisters.

4. A: How many people are there in your family? (有, 幾)

   B: There are six people in my family: my dad, my mom, two older brothers,
   a younger sister and I. (有)

5. A: What do your older brothers and older sisters do? (什麼)

▼▼▼

B: My older brothers and older sisters are all students.

6.*A:* My mom is a lawyer. My dad is a doctor. How about your mom and dad? (呢)

B: My mom is a lawyer, too. My dad is a teacher. (也)

7. Both my teacher and her teacher are Americans.

8. Neither Little Gao nor Little Zhang is Chinese.

Writing Practice

A. List your family members in Chinese.

B. To the best of your Chinese ability, tell what each of your family members does.

C. Write a paragraph describing the picture above.

One possible answer:

This is Little Zhang's picture. Little Zhang is my friend. He is Chinese. He is a teacher. He has three students.

LESSON 3 ▲ Dates and Time
第三課 ▲ 時間
Dì sān kè ▲ *Shíjiān*

Part One

DIALOGUE I: TAKING SOMEONE OUT TO EAT ON HIS/HER BIRTHDAY

I. Listening Comprehension

A. Textbook Dialogue I (True/False)

Quote the key sentence from the dialogue to support your answer.

( ) 1. Little Gao will be eighteen years old this year.

( ) 2. September 12 is Thursday.

( ) 3. Little Bai will treat Little Gao to a dinner on Thursday.

( ) 4. Little Gao is American. Therefore, he likes American food.

( ) 5. Little Bai refuses to eat American food.

( ) 6. They will have dinner together at 6:30 p.m.

B. Workbook Dialogue I (Multiple Choice)

( ) 1. Today's date is:

    a. May 10.   b. June 10.   c. October 5.   d. October 6.

( ) 2. What day is today?

    a. Thursday   b. Friday   c. Saturday   d. Sunday

( ) 3. What day is October 7?

    a. Thursday   b. Friday   c. Saturday   d. Sunday

C. Workbook Dialogue II (Multiple Choice)

( ) 1. What time does the man propose to meet?

    a. 6:30   b. 7:00   c. 7:30   d. 8:00

( ) 2. What time do they finally agree upon?

    a. 6:30   b. 7:00   c. 7:30   d. 8:00

(　) 3. What day are they going to meet?

　　a. Thursday　　b. Friday　　c. Saturday　　d. Sunday

II. Speaking Exercises

A. Answer the following questions in Chinese based on Textbook Dialogue I.

　　1. When is Little Gao's birthday?

　　2. How old is Little Gao?

　　3. Who is going to treat whom?

　　4. What is Little Gao's nationality?

　　5. What kind of dinner are they going to have?

　　6. What time is the dinner?

B. Tomorrow is your partner's birthday. Find out how old he/she is and offer to take him/her out to dinner. Ask him/her if he/she prefers Chinese or American food and decide upon the time for the dinner.

III. Reading Comprehension

A. Read the sentences and answer the questions. (Multiple Choice)

(　)1. 今天星期六，明天星期幾？

　　a. Thursday　　b. Friday　　c. Saturday　　d. Sunday

(　)2. 十月二號星期四，十月四號星期幾？

　　a. 星期四　　b. 星期五　　c. 星期六　　d. 星期日

B. Fill in the blanks below in English based on the calendar.

2005 年

九　月

22 日

星期一

The date on this calendar is _____.

The day of the week is _____.

Next month is _____.

The day after tomorrow is a _____.

C. Which of the following is the correct way to say "June 3, 1997" in Chinese? Circle the correct answer.

1. 六月三日一九九七年
2. 三日六月一九九七年
3. 六月一九九七年三日
4. 一九九七年六月三日

D. Read the following dialogue and answer the questions. (True/False)

小高： 小王，你喜歡吃中國飯還是美國飯？

小王： 我喜歡吃中國飯。

小高： 我請你吃中國飯怎麼樣？

小王： 太好了，謝謝。你星期幾請我吃飯？

小高： 星期六晚上，怎麼樣？

小王： 星期六晚上我很忙。

小高： 為什麼？

小王： 因為那天晚上我請李友吃晚飯。

Questions:

(   ) 1. Xiao Wang likes Chinese food better than American food.

(   ) 2. Xiao Gao offers to take Xiao Wang to dinner.

(   ) 3. Most likely Xiao Wang and Xiao Gao will not have dinner together on Saturday.

(   ) 4. Li You will treat Xiao Wang to dinner Saturday evening.

▼▼▼▼▼▼▼▼▼▼▼▼▼▼▼▼▼▼▼▼▼▼▼▼▼▼▼▼▼▼▼▼▼▼▼▼▼

IV. Writing & Grammar Exercises

Grammar and Usage

A. Write the following numbers using Chinese characters.

    1. 15 _____   2. 93 _____

    3. 47 _____   4. 62 _____

    5. Your phone number _____

B. Compose questions to elicit the following answers. Use 還是 *in each question.*

    Example: A: 王朋是中國人還是美國人？

               B: 王朋是中國人。

    1. A: _____ ？

      B: 我喜歡吃美國飯。

    2. A: _____ ？

      B: 小白是小高的同學。

    3. A: _____ ？

      B: 小張的爸爸是律師。

    5. A: _____ ？

      B: 李友是老師。

    6. A: _____ ？

      B: 星期二是我的生日。

C. Rearrange the following Chinese words into sentences, using the English sentences as clues.

1. 我 / 吃飯 / 今天 / 你 / 怎麼樣 / 晚上 / 請

How would it be if I take you out to dinner this evening?

2. 星期四 / 星期五 / 吃飯 / 我 / 你 / 還是 / 請

Is it Thursday or Friday that you are going to take me out to dinner?

3. 哥哥 / 小張 / 喜歡 / 他的 / 我 / 我 / 可是 / 不 / 喜歡

I do not like Little Zhang, but I like his older brother.

4. 美國人 / 美國飯 / 可是 / 他 / 不 / 喜歡 / 吃 / 是 / 他

He is American, but he does not like to eat American food.

Translation

Translate the following sentences into Chinese, using the words or phrases in parentheses.

1. What day of the week is June 3? (幾)

2. Whose birthday is August 7? (誰的)

3. What month and day is your dad's birthday? (幾)

4. How old is Little Gao (this year)? (多大)

5. Is Wang Peng Chinese or American? (還是)

6. Little Bai is American, but he likes to eat Chinese food. (可是)

7. In my family, there are Dad, Mom, a younger brother and I.

Writing Practice

A. *Write today's date in Chinese.*

B. *Write the current time in Chinese.*

Part Two

DIALOGUE II: INVITING SOMEONE TO DINNER

I. Listening Comprehension

A. Textbook Dialogue II (True/False)

Quote the key sentence from the dialogue to support your answer.

( ) 1. Wang Peng will not be free until 6:15.

( ) 2. Wang Peng will not be busy tomorrow.

( ) 3. Little Bai is inviting Wang Peng to dinner.

( ) 4. Tomorrow is Little Bai's birthday.

( ) 5. Wang Peng doesn't know Little Gao.

( ) 6. Little Li is Little Bai's schoolmate.

( ) 7. Wang Peng doesn't know Little Li.

B. Workbook Dialogue III (True/False)

Quote the key sentence from the dialogue to support your answer.

( ) 1. Both speakers in the dialogue are Chinese.

( ) 2. The man invites the woman to dinner because it will be his birthday tomorrow.

( ) 3. The man likes Chinese food.

( ) 4. The woman does not like Chinese food.

C. Workbook Dialogue IV (True/False)

Quote the key sentence from the dialogue to support your answer.

( ) 1. Today the woman is busy.

( ) 2. Today the man is not busy.

( ) 3. Tomorrow both the man and the woman will be very busy.

II. Speaking Exercises

A. *Answer the questions in Chinese based on Textbook Dialogue II.*

1. Why does Little Bai ask if Wang Peng is busy or not?

2. When is Wang Peng busy?

3. Who else will go out for dinner tomorrow with Little Bai and Wang Peng?

4. Does Little Bai know Little Li? How do you know?

B. *Invite a mutual friend to join you and your partner for dinner. Explain what the occasion is and who else will be there.*

C. *Your partner would like to take you out to dinner on your birthday, but you will be very busy that day. Suggest another day for the dinner and decide on a time.*

III. Reading Comprehension

A. *Write the following times in ordinary numeral notation (e.g., 1:00, 2:40, 3:10 p.m.).*

1. 三點鐘： _____

2. 兩點十分： _____

3. 六點五十分： _____

4. 晚上八點鐘： _____

5. 晚上九點一刻： _____

6. 晚上十一點半： _____

B. *Read the passage and answer the questions. (True/False)*

明天是小白的同學小高的生日。小白和他
姐姐請小高吃飯，因為小白的姐姐也認識
小高。小高是美國人，可是他喜歡吃中國
飯。明天晚上他們吃中國飯。

Questions:

( ) 1. Tomorrow is Little Bai's birthday.

( ) 2. Little Bai's sister knows Little Gao.

( ) 3. Little Gao and Little Bai are classmates.

( ) 4. Little Gao is Chinese.

( ) 5. Little Gao likes Chinese food.

( ) 6. Little Gao is going to pay for the dinner.

C. Read the passage and answer the questions. (True/False)

李小姐、白小姐和高先生是同學。今天是李小姐的生日，晚上六點半白小姐和高先生的妹妹請她吃晚飯，可是李小姐不認識高先生的妹妹。

Questions:

( ) 1. Miss Li and Miss Bai are classmates.

( ) 2. Miss Li is going to treat Miss Bai to dinner tonight.

( ) 3. Today is Miss Li's birthday.

( ) 4. Miss Li will not have dinner at home this evening.

( ) 5. Miss Li will see Mr. Gao at 6:30 p.m.

( ) 6. Miss Li and Mr. Gao's younger sister are close friends.

D. Read the following dialogue and answer the questions. (Multiple Choice)

小白： 今天是幾月幾號？

小李： 今天是二月二十八號。

小白： 是嗎？明天是我的生日。我的生日是二月二十九號。明天晚上我請你吃晚飯,怎麼樣？

▼▼▼▼▼▼▼▼▼▼▼▼▼▼▼▼▼▼▼▼▼▼▼▼▼▼▼▼▼▼▼▼▼▼

小李： 太好了,謝謝。可是明天不是二月二
十九號。

小白： 那明天是幾月幾號？

小李： 明天是三月一號。你今年沒有生日。

Questions:

( ) 1. Which of the following statements is true?

    a. Xiao Bai has been expecting her birthday all week.

    b. Xiao Bai almost failed to realize that her birthday was approaching.

    c. Xiao Li has been expecting Xiao Bai's birthday.

( ) 2. Tomorrow will be:

    a. February 28.   b. February 29.   c. March 1.

( ) 3. Which of the following statements is true?

    a. Xiao Bai has forgotten her birthday.

    b. Xiao Li gave the wrong date for tomorrow.

    c. Xiao Bai's birthday is off this year's calendar.

IV. Writing & Grammar Exercises

Grammar and Usage

A. Turn the following dates or time phrases into Chinese using Chinese characters.

1. November 12 _____

2. Friday evening _____

3. 7:00 this evening _____

4. 8:30 p.m. Saturday _____

5. quarter after nine _____

B. Complete the following exchanges.

1.A: 今天是幾月幾號？

B: ＿＿＿＿＿＿＿＿＿＿＿ 。

2.A: 你的生日是 ＿＿＿＿＿＿＿＿＿ ？

B: 我的生日是 ＿＿＿＿＿＿＿＿ 。

3.A: 你今年多大？

B: ＿＿＿＿＿＿＿＿＿ 。

4.A: 現在幾點鐘？

B: 現在 ＿＿＿ 點 ＿＿＿ 分 。

5.A: ＿＿＿＿＿＿＿＿＿＿＿ ？

B: 我五點三刻吃晚飯 。

C. Compose questions using the "A-not-A" form that would elicit the following answers.

Example: A: 王朋明天有沒有事？

B: 王朋明天沒有事 。

1.A: ＿＿＿＿＿＿＿＿＿＿ ？

B: 王先生是中國人 。

2.A: ＿＿＿＿＿＿＿＿＿＿ ？

B: 小高沒有弟弟 。

3.A: ＿＿＿＿＿＿＿＿＿＿ ？

B: 小高喜歡吃美國飯 。

4.A: ＿＿＿＿＿＿＿＿＿＿ ？

B: 王朋明天不忙 。

5. A: _____ ?

    B: 小張的爸爸不是醫生。

D. *Based on the text, answer the following questions with* 因為.

1. 小白為什麼請小高吃飯？

2. 小白為什麼不請小高吃中國飯？

3. 小白為什麼問王朋忙不忙？

4. 小白為什麼認識小李？

Translation

Translate the following sentences into Chinese, using the words or phrases in parentheses.

1. Who will you invite to dinner on Monday evening? (誰)

2. A: When are we having dinner tomorrow evening? (幾點鐘)

    B: Half past seven.

3. Little Zhang, will you be busy Thursday evening? (V + 不 + V)

4. We will treat our classmates to dinner. How does that sound? (怎麼樣)

5.*A:* Why are you busy today? (為什麼，因為)

   B: Because today is my mom's birthday.

6. I know my older brother's classmate, Little Zhang, but he doesn't know me.

Writing Practice

Write a note to your friend inviting him/her to have dinner with you tomorrow because it's your birthday.

LESSON 4 ▲ Hobbies

第四課 ▲ 愛好

Dì sì kè ▲ Àihào

Part One

DIALOGUE I: TALKING ABOUT HOBBIES

I. Listening Comprehension

A. Textbook Dialogue I (True/False)

Quote the key sentence from the dialogue to support your answer.

( ) 1. Little Gao likes watching TV.

( ) 2. Little Bai does a lot of reading every weekend.

( ) 3. Little Bai not only likes to sing, but also dance.

( ) 4. Little Gao likes playing ball and listening to music on weekends.

( ) 5. Both Little Gao and Little Bai like to dance.

( ) 6. Little Bai is treating Little Gao to a movie.

B. Workbook Dialogue I (Multiple Choice)

( ) 1. What does the man like to do the most?

    a. go to a concert   b. play ball

    c. go to the movies   d. go dancing

( ) 2. If the man and the woman decide to do something together, they will most likely go to:

    a. a movie.   b. a concert.

    c. a dance.   d. a ball game.

C. Workbook Dialogue II (Multiple Choice)

( ) 1. The man invites the woman to:

    a. a dinner.   b. a movie.

    c. a dance.   d. a concert.

( ) 2. The man gives the invitation because:

   a. the woman has invited him to a dinner before.

   b. the woman has invited him to a concert before.

   c. tomorrow is his birthday.

   d. tomorrow is her birthday.

( ) 3. Which of the following statements is true?

   a. The woman doesn't accept the invitation although she will not be
      busy tomorrow.

   b. The woman doesn't accept the invitation because she'll be busy
      tomorrow.

   c. The woman accepts the invitation although she'll be busy
      tomorrow.

   d. The woman accepts the invitation because she will not be busy
      tomorrow.

II. Speaking Exercises

A. Answer the questions in Chinese based on Textbook Dialogue I.

   1. What does Little Gao like to do on weekends?
   2. What does Little Bai like to do on weekends?
   3. What will Little Bai and Little Gao do tonight?
   4. Who is treating tonight?
   5. Who took whom to dinner yesterday?

*B. Discuss your interests and hobbies with your friends, and then make an appointment with them based on your
common interests.*

III. Reading Comprehension

A. Match the phrases with the appropriate pictures.

1. 打球 ( )   2. 跳舞 ( )   3. 唱歌 ( )

4. 聽音樂 ( )   5. 看電視 ( )

B. Read the passage and answer the questions. (True/False)

> 昨天是張律師的生日，他的同學王先生昨
> 天晚上請他吃晚飯。因為王先生請張律師
> 吃飯，所以張律師這個週末請王先生去看
> 一個外國電影。

Questions:

( ) 1. Yesterday was Lawyer Wang's birthday.

( ) 2. Yesterday Lawyer Zhang didn't have dinner at home.

( ) 3. Yesterday Mr. Wang and Lawyer Zhang went to see a foreign movie.

( ) 4. Mr. Wang wants to take Lawyer Zhang to a movie because Lawyer Zhang took him out to dinner.

C. *Read the following dialogue and answer the questions. (True/False)*

昨天是小白的生日，所以他昨天晚上請王朋，李友和張英去跳舞。李友和張英都是女孩子。李友喜歡和王朋跳舞。小白請張英跳舞，可是張英不喜歡跳舞，所以昨天晚上小白和張英都沒跳舞。

Questions:

（　）1. Little Bai invited three friends yesterday evening to celebrate his birthday.

（　）2. Wang Peng danced with both girls.

（　）3. Li You preferred to dance with Wang Peng.

（　）4. Xiao Bai danced for several hours.

D. *Read the passage and answer the following questions in English.*

我哥哥認識一個女孩子，她的名字叫李明英。李小姐今年二十歲，是大學生。我哥哥很喜歡她，常常請她吃晚飯。週末兩個人喜歡去跳舞、看電影。可是李小姐的爸爸和媽媽不喜歡我哥哥。因為我哥哥今年三十八歲，有兩個女兒。我也不喜歡他們兩個人做男女朋友，因為李小姐是我的同學。

Questions:

1. What are the three things that we know about Miss Li?

2. What do the two lovebirds like to do on weekends?

3. What are the two reasons that Ms. Li's parents don't like their daughter dating the narrator's brother?

4. What's the narrator's attitude toward the relationship? Why does she feel this way?

IV. Writing & Grammar Exercises

Grammar and Usage

Use a word or phrase from each of the four following groups to make four sentences based on the Chinese word order of Subject + Time + Verb + Object.

Group 1: 美國飯，球，音樂，電影

Group 2: 明天晚上，這個週末，星期四，今天

Group 3: 去看，去聽，去打，去吃

Group 4: 我們，我爸爸媽媽，小白和小高，王朋和李友

1. _____ 。

2. _____ 。

3. _____ 。

4. _____ 。

▼▼

Translation

Translate the following sentences into Chinese using the words or phrases in parentheses.

1. Do you like to dance on weekends? (V + 不 + V)

2. I often invite my classmates to go to see foreign movies. (請...去 + V)

3. I like singing and listening to music. Sometimes I also like reading.

4. Because it was your treat yesterday, I'll take you to dinner tomorrow. (因為...所以)

5.*A:* You like to sing, right?

   B: Yes, I sing very often.

6. Is tomorrow your younger brother's birthday (or not)? (V + 不 + V)

Writing Practice

List your hobbies in Chinese.

Part Two

DIALOGUE II: INVITING SOMEONE TO PLAY BALL

I. Listening Comprehension

A. Textbook Dialogue II (True/False)

Quote the key sentence from the dialogue to support your answer.

( ) 1. Little Zhang does not like playing ball.

( ) 2. Wang Peng wants to play ball this weekend.

( ) 3. Little Zhang is very interested in movies.

( ) 4. Wang Peng is going out to eat with Little Zhang.

( ) 5. Little Zhang likes to sleep.

( ) 6. In the end Wang Peng gives up the idea of going out with Little Zhang.

B. Workbook Dialogue III (True/False)

Quote the key sentence from the dialogue to support your answer.

( ) 1. The woman doesn't like Chinese movies because her Chinese is not good enough.

( ) 2. The woman prefers American movies over Chinese movies.

( ) 3. The man invites the woman to an American movie at the end of the conversation.

C. Workbook Dialogue IV (True/False)

Quote the key sentence from the dialogue to support your answer.

( ) 1. The woman invites the man to a concert.

( ) 2. The man is interested in sports.

( ) 3. The man invites the woman to go dancing.

D. Workbook Narrative (Multiple Choice)

(   ) 1. The speaker probably spends most of his spare time:

    a. in movie theaters

    b. in concert halls.

    c. in front of a TV set

    d. in a library.

(   ) 2. According to the speaker, Wang Peng loves:

    a. movies and TV.

    b. dancing and reading.

    c. dancing and music.

    d. reading only.

(   ) 3. Which of the following statements is true about the speaker and Wang Peng?

    a. Wang Peng likes to read.

    b. The speaker likes to watch TV.

    c. Both the speaker and Wang Peng like to dance.

    d. Wang Peng and the speaker are classmates.

II. Speaking Exercises

A. Answer the questions in Chinese based on Textbook Dialogue II.

1. Did Wang Peng see Little Zhang yesterday? How do you know?

2. Does Little Zhang want to play ball? Why?

3. Does Little Zhang want to go to the movies? Why?

4. What does Little Zhang like to do?

5. What did Wang Peng finally decide to do this weekend?

B. Your partner is inviting you to do something. Keep rejecting the suggestions he/she makes and give reasons why you do not like those activities.

III. Reading Comprehension

A. *Match the questions on the left with the appropriate replies on the right. Write down the letter in the parentheses.*

( ) 1. 你叫什麼名字？　　　　　A. 我明天不忙。

( ) 2. 這是你弟弟嗎？　　　　　B. 今天晚上我很忙。

( ) 3. 你明天忙不忙？　　　　　C. 我想看一個外國電影。

( ) 4. 你認識小張嗎？　　　　　D. 不,這是我哥哥。

( ) 5. 你喜歡聽音樂嗎？　　　　E. 因為我喜歡吃美國飯。

( ) 6. 為什麼你請我看電影？　　F. 認識，他是我同學。

( ) 7. 為什麼我們不吃中國飯？　G. 我叫王朋。

( ) 8. 我們去打球，好嗎？　　　H. 我覺得聽音樂沒有意思。

( ) 9. 這個週末你做什麼？　　　I. 我不想打球。

( )10. 今天晚上我去找你，　　　J. 因為今天是你的生日。
　　　好嗎？

B. *Read the passage and answer the questions. (Multiple Choice)*

小王和小李是同學。小王是中國人，他喜歡打球、看電視和看書。小李是美國人，她喜歡聽音樂、唱歌和跳舞。他們都喜歡看電影，可是小王只喜歡看美國電影，小李覺得美國電影沒有意思，她只喜歡看外國電影。她覺得中國電影很有意思。

( ) 1. What activities does Little Wang enjoy?

　　a. watching TV and listening to music

　　b. watching Chinese movies and dancing

　　c. watching American movies and singing

　　d. playing ball and reading

（　）2. What does Little Li like to do?

    a. watch TV and listen to music

    b. watch Chinese movies and dance

    c. watch American movies and dance

    d. play ball and read

（　）3. Which of the following statements is true?

    a. Little Wang and Little Li both like to watch TV.

    b. Little Wang is American and he likes American movies.

    c. Little Li is Chinese and she likes American movies.

    d. Little Wang and Little Li know each other.

（　）4. If Little Wang and Little Li want to do something they are both interested in, where can they go together?

    a. a movie theater   b. a library

    c. a dancing party   d. none of the above

C. Read the following dialogue and answer the questions. (True/False)

小張：你喜歡看美國電影還是外國電影？

老李：我不喜歡看美國電影，也不喜歡看外國電影。

小張：你覺得中國音樂有意思還是美國音樂有意思？

老李：我覺得中國音樂和美國音樂都沒有意思。

小張：你常常看中文書還是英文書？

老李：我不看中文書，也不看英文書。

小張：那你喜歡吃中國飯還是美國飯？

老李：中國飯和美國飯我都喜歡吃。

▼▼▼▼▼▼▼▼▼▼▼▼▼▼▼▼▼▼▼▼▼▼▼▼▼▼▼▼▼▼▼

Questions:

(　) 1. This conversation most likely takes place in the United States.

(　) 2. Old Li does not like American movies, but likes foreign ones.

(　) 3. Old Li feels that both Chinese music and American music are boring.

(　) 4. When Old Li reads, the book must be in a language other than English or Chinese.

(　) 5. It seems Old Li does not like anything American or Chinese.

IV. Writing & Grammar Exercises

Grammar and Usage

A. *Use* "(沒)有意思" *to complete the following dialogues.*

1.A: 你覺得昨天的電影＿＿＿＿＿＿＿嗎？

B: 不，我覺得＿＿＿＿＿＿。

2.A: 你想去看中國電影嗎？

B: 不想。我＿＿＿＿＿＿。

3.A: 你為什麼不聽中國音樂？

B: 因為＿＿＿＿＿＿。

4.A: 今天晚上的電視都很＿＿＿＿＿＿，
我們去唱歌，好不好？

B: 我不想去，我＿＿＿＿＿＿。

B. *Use* "因為...所以" *to answer the following questions.*

1.A: 小高為什麼請小白看電影？

B: ＿＿＿＿＿＿＿＿＿＿＿＿＿＿＿＿。

2.A: 小張為什麼不想去打球？

B: ＿＿＿＿＿＿＿＿＿＿＿＿＿＿＿＿。

3.A: 小張為什麼不想去看電影？

B: _____ 。

C. *Complete the following exchanges.*

1.A: 你週末常常做什麼？

B: _____ 。

2.A: 你喜歡看美國電影還是外國電影？

B: _____ 。

3.A: 星期一晚上的電影有意思還是星期六晚
　　 上的電影有意思？

B: _____ 。

4.A: 你今天晚上幾點鐘睡覺？

B: _____ 。

5.A: 你覺得看書有意思還是看電視有意思？

B: _____ 。

Translation

Translate the following sentences into Chinese using the words or phrases in parentheses.

1. Little Zhang, long time no see.

2. Do you feel like going to play ball this weekend? (V+ 不 +V ，去 +V)

3. I don't like reading. I only like eating, watching TV and sleeping. (只)

4. I think this foreign movie is very interesting. (有意思)

5. Then forget it. I'll go to bed. (去)

6. I am very busy today. I don't want to go to see the movie. (想)

7. I don't like foreign movies. I only like American movies. (只)

8. You don't feel like going to the movies. Then let's go dancing. How's that sound?

Writing Practice

Describe in detail what you did last weekend.

LESSON 5 ▲ Visiting Friends
第五課 ▲ 看朋友
Dì wǔ kè ▲ *Kàn péngyou*

Part One

DIALOGUE: VISITING A FRIEND'S HOME

I. Listening Comprehension

A. Textbook Dialogue (True/False)

Quote the key sentence from the dialogue to support your answer.

( ) 1. Wang Peng and Li You had met Little Gao's older sister before.

( ) 2. Li You was very happy to meet Little Gao's younger sister.

( ) 3. Li You thought that Little Gao's house was nice and big.

( ) 4. Little Gao's older sister works in a restaurant.

( ) 5. Li You did not drink beer.

( ) 6. Little Gao's sister gave Li You a cola.

( ) 7. Li You did not drink anything at Little Gao's house.

B. Workbook Dialogue I (True/False)

Quote the key sentence from the dialogue to support your answer.

( ) 1. The man and the woman run into each other in a library.

( ) 2. The man and the woman have never met each other before.

( ) 3. The man is looking for his younger brother.

C. Workbook Dialogue II (Multiple Choice)

( ) 1. The dialogue most likely occurs in:

    a. a car.   b. a house.

    c. a library.   d. a concert hall.

(   ) 2. Which of the following statements about the woman is true?

    a. She doesn't like TV in general but she likes what is on TV tonight.

    b. She doesn't like TV in general and she likes what is on TV tonight even less.

    c. She likes TV in general but she doesn't like what is on TV tonight.

    d. She likes TV in general and she particularly likes what is on TV tonight.

(   ) 3. What will they most likely do for the rest of the evening?

    a. watch TV   b. listen to American music

    c. read an American novel   d. listen to Chinese music

D. Workbook Dialogue III (Multiple Choice)

(   ) 1. Which of the following is the correct order of the woman's preferences?

    a. coffee, tea   b. beer, coffee

    c. coffee, beer   d. tea, coffee

(   ) 2. Which beverage does the man not have?

    a. tea   b. beer

    c. cola   d. coffee

(   ) 3. Which beverage does the woman finally get?

    a. tea   b. beer

    c. cola   d. coffee

II. Speaking Exercises

A. Answer the questions in Chinese based on the Textbook Dialogue.

1. Who went to Little Gao's house?

2. Did Wang Peng and Li You know Little Gao's older sister before?

3. What is Little Gao's older sister's name?

4. How is Little Gao's house?

5. Where does Little Gao's older sister work?

6. What did Wang Peng want to drink?

7. Why did Li You ask for a glass of water?

B. *This picture depicts a scene from Dialogue I of this lesson. Act it out with some of your classmates.*

C. *You are talking with a classmate's brother/sister for the first time. Find out if he/she is a student, where he/she works, and what his/her hobbies are.*

D. *You are visiting a friend's home. Compliment your friend on the home. Your friend offers you something to drink, so you ask for a glass of water.*

III. Reading Comprehension

A. *Read the following description carefully and match each of the names with the proper beverage by placing the letters in the appropriate parentheses.*

> 小高、小張和王朋都是同學，小高今年
> 十九歲，小張今年二十歲，王朋今年二
> 十一歲。小高不喜歡喝茶，小張不喝可
> 樂，王朋喜歡喝咖啡、啤酒，可是不喜
> 歡喝茶。

( )1. 小高   a. 茶

( )2. 小張   b. 啤酒

( )3. 王朋   c. 可樂

▼▼▼▼▼▼▼▼▼▼▼▼▼▼▼▼▼▼▼▼▼▼▼▼▼▼▼▼▼▼▼▼▼▼▼

B. Read the following dialogue and answer the questions. (True/False)

（王亮和李樂都是美國學生。他們都學中文。）

王亮：你想喝點兒什麼？

李樂：我要啤酒。

王亮：我不可以給你啤酒，因為你今年只
　　　有十九歲。

李樂：對，我今年十九歲，可是我為什麼
　　　不可以喝啤酒？啤酒是 cola，對不
　　　對？

王亮：不對， cola 中文是可樂。

李樂：是嗎？那請你給我一杯可樂吧。

王亮：好吧。

Questions:

　　（　）1. The two people know each other.

　　（　）2. The dialogue most likely occurred in Li Le's apartment.

　　（　）3. Li Le knew that he was too young to drink beer, but he asked for it
　　　　　anyway.

　　（　）4. Wang Liang's Chinese is probably better than Li Le's.

　　（　）5. Finally, Li Le got what he actually wanted.

IV. Writing & Grammar Exercises

Grammar and Usage

A. Answer the following questions.

1.A: 你常常在家看書還是在學校看書？

　　B: _____ 。

2.A: 你爸爸媽媽在哪兒工作？

B: _____ 。

3.A: 你喜歡喝茶還是喜歡喝咖啡？

B: _____ 。

4.A: 你爸爸喜歡喝美國啤酒還是喜歡喝外國
啤酒？

B: _____ 。

B. *Use each group of words to make an interrogative sentence, a positive sentence, and a negative sentence.*

Example: 小高家/大

A. 小高家大不大？

B. 小高家很大。

C. 小高家不大。

1.這個醫生/好

A. _____ ？

B. _____ 。

C. _____ 。

2. 小白的妹妹/漂亮

A. _____ ？

B. _____ 。

C. _____ 。

3. 張律師/高興

A. _____ ？

B. _____ 。

C. _____ 。

4. 那個電影/有意思

A. _____ ?

B. _____ 。

C. _____ 。

Translation

Translate the following sentences into Chinese, using the words or phrases in parentheses.

1. Let me introduce you. This is my classmate.

2. Very pleased to meet you. (認識)

3. Little Gao's home is very big and also very beautiful. (Adj.)

4.*A:* Where do you work? (在，哪兒)

B: I work at a school.

5. Would you like to have some coffee? (點兒)

6. Would you like to drink cola or beer? (還是)

7. *A:* Please give me a cup of coffee.

   B: Sorry. We don't have coffee.

8. Come in quickly. Sit down please.

Writing Practice

List what you like to drink in Chinese.

Part Two

NARRATIVE: AT A FRIEND'S HOUSE

I. Listening Comprehension

A. Textbook Narrative (True/False)

Quote the key sentence from the dialogue to support your answer.

(   ) 1. Little Gao's older sister works in a library.

(   ) 2. Wang Peng had two glasses of beer at Little Gao's house.

(   ) 3. Li You did not drink beer at Little Gao's house.

(   ) 4. Wang Peng and Li You chatted and watched TV with Little Gao's sister last night.

(   ) 5. Wang Peng and Li You left Little Gao's house at noon.

B. *Workbook Narrative I (True/False)*

Quote the key sentence from the dialogue to support your answer.

( ) 1. The speaker thinks that Little Bai and Little Li are old friends.

( ) 2. The three people are most likely at the speaker's place.

( ) 3. Little Bai told Little Li that he works in the library.

C. *Workbook Narrative II (Multiple Choice)*

( ) 1. Where did they spend last Saturday evening? They were:

a. at Little Bai's place.   b. at Little Gao's place.

c. at Little Li's place.   d. at Little Bai's brother's place.

( ) 2. What did Little Bai's brother do at the party? He was:

a. drinking.   b. watching TV.

c. chatting.   d. dancing.

( ) 3. Little Bai spent most of the evening:

a. drinking and watching TV.   b. chatting and watching TV.

c. drinking and chatting.   d. drinking, chatting and watching TV.

II. Speaking Exercises

A. *Answer the questions in Chinese based on the Textbook Narrative.*

1. Why did Wang Peng and Li You go to Little Gao's house?

2. Is Little Gao's older sister a teacher? Explain.

3. What did Wang Peng drink? How much?

4. What did Wang Peng and Li You do at Little Gao's house?

5. When did Wang Peng and Li You go home?

B. *Explain in Chinese that you went to a friend's house last night. Your friend works at the school library. You chatted and watched TV together and did not return home until 11:30 p.m.*

III. Reading Comprehension

A. Read the following note and answer the questions in English.

小張：

　明天晚上七點半學校有一個中國電
影，我們一起去看，好嗎？請你晚上
來找我。

　　　　　小高

　　　　　七月五日晚上九點半

1. Who wrote the note?

2. What time is the movie?

3. Where is the movie?

4. What date is the movie?

5. When was the note written?

B. Read the passage and answer the questions. (Multiple Choice)

昨天是小李的生日，小李請了小高、小張
和王朋三個同學去她家吃飯。他們七點鐘
吃晚飯。小李的家很大，也很漂亮。小李
的爸爸是老師，他很有意思。小李的媽媽
是醫生，昨天很忙，九點才回家吃晚飯。
小李的哥哥和姐姐都不在家吃飯。王朋和
小李的爸爸媽媽一起喝茶、聊天。小高、
小張和小李一起喝可樂、看電視。小高、
小張和王朋十一點才回家。

( ) 1. Where did Little Gao go last night?

    a. Little Li's home   b. Little Zhang's home

    c. Wang Peng's home   d. His own home

( ) 2. Who was late for dinner last night?

    a. Little Gao   b. Little Zhang

    c. Little Li's father   d. Little Li's mother

( ) 3. Which of the following statements is true?

    a. Little Li's mother is a teacher.

    b. Little Li's father is an interesting person.

    c. Little Li's brother and sister were home last night.

    d. Wang Peng talked with Little Li all evening.

C. Read the passage and answer the questions. (True/False)

今天小高去找他的同學小張，小張的妹妹
也在家。可是小高不認識小張的妹妹。小
張介紹了一下。小張的妹妹也是他們學校

的學生。她很漂亮，喜歡唱歌和看書。這個週末小高想請小張的妹妹去喝咖啡、看電影。

Questions:

(　) 1. Little Gao has met Little Zhang's sister before.
(　) 2. Little Gao and Little Zhang's sister attend the same school.
(　) 3. Little Gao's sister likes to dance.
(　) 4. Little Gao would like to invite Little Zhang and his sister to see a movie this weekend.

IV. Writing & Grammar Exercises

Grammar and Usage

A. Answer the following questions based on your own situation.

1. 你喜歡去同學家玩嗎？為什麼？

2. 你喜歡喝茶、可樂、咖啡還是啤酒？為什麼？

3. 你喜歡在哪兒看書？

4. 你和你的同學常常一起做什麼？

5. 昨天晚上你去沒去朋友家玩兒？

B. *Change the following sentences from the positive to the negative.*

　　　　Example: A: 我昨天晚上看電視了。

　　　　　　　→ B: 我昨天晚上沒(有)看電視。

1.A: 今天他打球了。

　　B: _____ 。

2.A: 我昨天晚上去小高家了。

　　B: _____ 。

3.A: 星期五是小高的生日，王朋喝啤酒了。

　　B: _____ 。

4.A: 星期三他去圖書館了。

　　B: _____ 。

C. *Answer the following questions in both the positive and the negative forms.*

　　　　Example:　A: 你昨天晚上跳舞了嗎？

　　　　　　　→ B1: 我昨天晚上跳舞了。

　　　　　　　→ B2: 我昨天晚上沒(有)跳舞。

1.A: 小李昨天晚上喝茶了嗎？

　　B1: _____ 。

　　B2: _____ 。

2.A: 你今天喝咖啡了嗎？

　　B1: _____ 。

　　B2: _____ 。

3.A: 小白星期四回家了嗎？

    B1: _____ 。

    B2: _____ 。

4.A: 星期六小高去朋友家玩了嗎？

    B1: _____ 。

    B2: _____ 。

Translation

Translate the following sentences into Chinese, using the words or phrases in parentheses.

1. We got acquainted with Little Gao's older sister at the library. (在)

2. Last night they drank tea and chatted together. (聊天)

3. Last night Little Zhang drank four cups of coffee. (了, measure word)

4. Little Bai does not like beer. He only drank two glasses of cola.

5.A: Why did you get home as late as twelve? (才)

    B: Because I went to see a foreign movie.

6. Last night Wang Peng went to Li You's home for a visit. He met Li You's
   older sister.

7. Let's go home! (吧)

8. Let's eat dinner! (吧)

Writing Practice

A. *Describe a recent visit to your friend's house. Make sure that you mention what you did and what you drank.*

B. *Translate the following note into Chinese.*

Yesterday evening I went to the library to read. In the library I met a classmate. We read together. I didn't go home until eleven o'clock.

LESSON 6 ▲ Making Appointments
第六課 ▲ 約時間
Dì liù kè ▲ *Yuē shíjiān*

Part One

DIALOGUE I: CALLING ONE'S TEACHER

I. Listening Comprehension

A. Textbook Dialogue I (Multiple Choice)

(   ) 1. Why does Li You call Teacher Wang?

    a. Li You cannot come to school, because she is sick.

    b. Li You wants to ask some questions.

    c. Li You wants to know where Teacher Wang's office is.

    d. Li You wants to know where the meeting is.

(   ) 2. What is Teacher Wang going to do this afternoon?

    a. teach two classes   b. go home early

    c. attend a meeting   d. go to a doctor's office

(   ) 3. How many classes will Teacher Wang teach tomorrow morning?

    a. 1   b. 2

    c. 3   d. 4

(   ) 4. What will Teacher Wang be doing at 3:30 tomorrow afternoon?

    a. attending a meeting   b. giving an exam

    c. working in his office   d. seeing a doctor

(   ) 5. Where is Li You going to meet Teacher Wang?

    a. in Teacher Wang's office   b. in the classroom

    c. in the meeting room   d. in the library

(   ) 6. When will Li You meet with Teacher Wang tomorrow?

    a. 9:00 a.m.   b. 10:30 a.m.

    c. 3:00 p.m.   d. 4:30 p.m.

B. Workbook Dialogue I (True/False)

Quote the key sentence from the dialogue to support your answer.

( ) 1. The woman in the dialogue is the man's sister.

( ) 2. The telephone call was originally not meant for the woman.

( ) 3. There is going to be a Chinese film tonight.

( ) 4. The woman will most likely stay home tonight.

C. Workbook Dialogue II (Multiple Choice)

( ) 1. Which of the following statements is true?

a. The woman invites the man to a dinner party at her home.

b. The woman invites the man to a dance at her home.

c. The woman hopes to go to the dinner party at the man's home.

d. The woman hopes to go to the dance at the man's home.

( ) 2. Why can't the man go?

a. He is giving a party.

b. He has to prepare for a test.

c. He has another dinner party to go to.

d. He has another dance to go to.

II. Speaking Exercises

A. Answer the questions in Chinese based on Textbook Dialogue I.

1. Why did Li You call Teacher Wang?

2. Will Teacher Wang be free this afternoon? Explain.

3. Will Teacher Wang be free tomorrow morning? Explain.

4. What will Teacher Wang do at three o'clock tomorrow afternoon?

5. When will Li You go to visit Teacher Wang?

6. Where will Teacher Wang and Li You meet?

B. You are on the phone with your teacher. You would like to make an appointment with him/her. Your teacher happens to be busy at the time you suggest. Ask your teacher when he/she will be available. Decide on a time and place to meet.

III. Reading Comprehension

A. Match the responses on the left with the expressions on the right. Write the appropriate letter in the parentheses.

( )1. 認識你們我也很高興。

( )2. 不客氣。

( )3. 再見。

( )4. 對不起，我不喝酒。

( )5. 對不起，小白不在。

( )6. 對不起，我今天下午
要開會。

( )7. 對不起，我明天要
考試。

( )8. 我是王朋。

A. 你是哪位？

B. 我們今天晚上去跳舞，
好嗎？

C. 喝點兒酒，怎麼樣？

D. 喂，請問小白在嗎？

E. 認識你很高興。

F. 謝謝。

G. 明天見。

H. 今天下午我來找你，
好嗎？

B. Read the following schedule and answer the questions. (True/False)

這是小王今天要做的事：

8:00	中文課
10:00	去白老師辦公室
14:30	看王醫生
16:00	開會
18:00	和小李吃飯
20:30	請小李喝咖啡
23:15	和小張去學校看電影

Questions:

( )1. 小王今天只有一節課。

( )2. 小王要和小李一起吃午飯。

( )3. 小王上午要找白老師。

( )4. 今天晚上小李要請小王喝咖啡。

( )5. 今天晚上小王要晚上十二點以後才回家。

C. Read the passage and answer the questions. (True/False)

李友是張老師的學生。今天上午李友給張老師打電話，因為她下個星期考試，想問張老師幾個問題。可是張老師今天下午有課，沒有時間見李友。張老師明天上午要開會，下午有兩節課，三點半以後才有空。李友可以四點以後到辦公室去找他。

Questions:

( )1. 今天上午張老師給李友打電話了。

( )2. 李友想請張老師給她考試。

( )3. 張老師今天下午不忙。

( )4. 張老師明天下午兩點半要上課。

( )5. 李友明天四點鐘以後可以去問張老師
幾個問題。

D. Read the following dialogue and answer the questions.

(李友給王朋打電話。李友問了王朋幾個問
題。)

王朋： 還有別的問題嗎？

李友： 我還有一個問題。

王朋： 你問吧。

李友： 你明天下午有空嗎？

王朋： 我明天下午要開會。

李友： 明天晚上呢？

王朋： 我明天晚上也沒有時間。我想請一
位女孩子去聽音樂。

李友： 那算了。

王朋： 你認識那個女孩子。

李友： 是嗎？她叫什麼名字？

王朋： 她姓李，叫李友。

Questions:

(True/False)

(   ) 1. Li You's schedule for tomorrow seems quite flexible.

(   ) 2. Wang Peng hopes to see Li You tomorrow.

(   ) 3. Li You does not know the girl Wang Peng mentioned.

(Multiple Choice)

(   ) 4. The conversation mostly likely took place:

     a. in a movie theater.

     b. at a concert.

     c. in a dorm.

(   ) 5. On hearing of Wang Peng's plan for tomorrow evening, Li You must be:

     a. first disappointed and then very happy.

     b. first very happy and then disappointed.

     c. neither happy nor disappointed.

IV. Writing & Grammar Exercises

Grammar and Usage

A. Fill in the blanks with appropriate measure words.

1. 兩 _____ 問題

2. 您是哪 _____ ？

3. 三 _____ 課

4. 四 _____ 茶 (cup)

5. 五 _____ 啤酒 (bottle)

B. Use 要是 to answer the following questions.

1. 要是你明天沒課，你想做什麼？

2. 要是今天你們的老師請你們吃飯，你想吃美國飯還是吃中國飯？

3. 要是你明天考試，你想在圖書館還是在家看書？

4. 要是你有空，你想去看電影還是想去打球？

Translation

Translate the following sentences into Chinese, using the words or phrases in parentheses.

1. This morning my teacher called me. (給, 了)

2. Teacher, are you free this weekend? I'd like to invite you to dinner. (有 時間，請)

3. When will you be free this weekend? (有空兒)

4. This afternoon I went to look for Teacher Zhang, but he wasn't in his office. (可是，在)

5. Tomorrow afternoon I have two classes. I won't be free until after three thirty. (以後，才)

6. This afternoon I have to give an exam to the first-year class. (要)

7. If it's convenient for you, I will go to your office at 4:00 p.m. Is that all right? (要是，去)

8. Don't go to his office. (別)

9. Buy you dinner? No problem!

10.*A:* Hello. Is Little Bai there?

B: This is he. Who is this?

Writing Practice

List the things that you need to do today. Don't forget to include the times.

Part Two

DIALOGUE II: CALLING A FRIEND FOR HELP

I. Listening Comprehension

A. Textbook Dialogue II (True/False)

Quote the key sentence from the dialogue to support your answer.

      (   ) 1. Li You is returning Wang Peng's phone call.

      (   ) 2. Li You has an examination next week.

      (   ) 3. Li You is asking Wang Peng to practice Chinese with her.

      (   ) 4. Wang Peng is inviting Li You to have coffee.

      (   ) 5. Wang Peng is going to have dinner with Li You this evening.

      (   ) 6. Wang Peng does not know exactly when he is going to call Li You.

B. Listen to Dialogue II very carefully to see if you can locate the section depicted by the illustration below.

C. Workbook Dialogue III (True/False)

Quote the key sentence from the dialogue to support your answer.

(   ) 1. Tomorrow will be Friday.

(   ) 2. Li You cannot go for the dinner tomorrow because she will be busy.

(   ) 3. Li You will be practicing Chinese this evening.

(   ) 4. Wang Peng promises to help Li You with her Chinese tomorrow at 6:00 p.m.

D. Workbook Dialogue IV (True/False)

Quote the key sentence from the dialogue to support your answer.

(   ) 1. Wang Peng cannot help Li You practice Chinese because he has classes tomorrow afternoon.

(   ) 2. Wang Peng asks Miss Bai to help Li You with her Chinese.

(   ) 3. Miss Bai and Li You will meet at 2:00 p.m. tomorrow in the library.

II. Speaking Exercises

A. Answer the questions in Chinese based on Textbook Dialogue II.

1. Why did Li You call Wang Peng? Please explain.

2. Why did Wang Peng ask Li You to invite him for coffee?

3. What will Wang Peng do tonight?

4. When will Wang Peng call Li You?

5. Will Li You go to see a movie tonight? Please explain.

B. You are calling a friend to ask for a favor and you promise to treat him/her to something in return. You would like to meet him/her tonight, but he/she is going to see a movie and does not know when he/she will be back. He/she promises that he/she will give you a call when he/she comes back.

C. You are calling a friend to ask a favor. Your friend is willing to help you. Decide on a time and place to meet, and promise that you will take your friend out to a foreign movie.

III. Reading Comprehension

A. Read this note and answer the following questions. (Multiple Choice)

小高：

小張下午打電話給你了。他想請你星
期四下午幫他練習中文，不知道你有
沒有空。回來以後給他打電話，他的
電話是 324-6597。

姐姐

三月八號(星期二)下午三點

Questions:

(　) 1. Who wrote the note?

    a. 小高。   b. 小張。

    c. 小高的姐姐。   d. 小張的姐姐。

(　) 2. Which of the following is true?

    a. 小張星期四下午給小高打了一個電
    話。
    b. 小高知道星期四下午要幫小張練習說
    中文。
    c. 小高的姐姐請小高回來以後給小張打
    電話。
    d. 小高的姐姐給小張打了一個電話。

(　) 3. Which of the following is true?

    a. 明天是星期四。
    b. 明天是三月九號。

c.三月八號是星期四。

d.三月十號是星期二。

B. Authentic Materials

Below is a page of Little Gao's appointment book. Take a look at the things that he plans to do this week and answer the following questions in English.

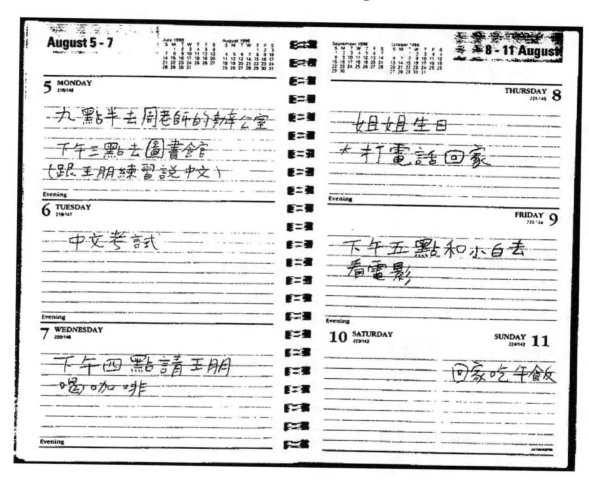

Questions:

1.他星期天在哪兒吃飯？

2.他什麼時候考中文？

3. 他和王朋在哪兒練習中文？

4. 他姐姐的生日是幾月幾號？

5. 他星期五下午有什麼事？

6. 他請誰喝咖啡？

7. 他們星期幾喝咖啡？

8. 他們幾點鐘喝咖啡？

9. 他星期天中午在哪兒？

C. Read the passage and answer the questions. (True/False)

小張今天很忙，上午有四節課，中午和同
學一起吃飯，下午在圖書館看書，和小李
練習中文，晚上到小白的學校去看電影，
十一點才回家。因為明天他有兩個考試，
所以今天晚上他沒有時間睡覺。

Questions:

( )1. 小張今天沒有時間吃午飯。

( )2. 小張今天下午沒有課。

( )3. 小張今天和小李在圖書館練習中文。

( )4. 小白不是小張學校的學生。

( )5. 今天晚上十點半小張不在家。

( )6. 因為小張要看電影，所以他今天晚上沒有時間睡覺。

D. Read the following note and answer the questions.

王朋：

　　李友今天上午十點鐘給你打電話了。她昨天晚上才知道星期五下午有中文考試，所以她今天晚上不和你去聽音樂。要是你有空，她想今天下午請你幫她練習中文，她考試以後請你看電影。你回來以後給她打一個電話吧。

小高

十二點半

Questions:

(True/False)

( ) 1. Xiao Gao is most likely Wang Peng's roommate.

( ) 2. Wang Peng was not in at 10:00 a.m. but was back around 12:25 p.m.

( ) 3. At 4:00 p.m. yesterday Li You still planned to go to the concert.

( ) 4. We do not know when Wang Peng will call Li You back.

( ) 5. Li You was certain that Wang Peng would be available this afternoon.

(Multiple Choice)

( ) 6. Which of the statements is true?

    a. Li You had been told last Friday that there would be an exam last night.

    b. Li You was told yesterday evening that there would be an exam on Friday.

    c. Li You was told that yesterday evening's exam was postponed till Friday.

( ) 7. Li You hopes to take Wang Peng to a movie this:

    a. Wednesday evening.

    b. Thursday evening.

    c. Friday evening.

IV. Writing & Grammar Exercises

Grammar and Usage

A. Answer the following questions using the words in parentheses and 得 *(děi).*

    Example: 為什麼今天晚上你不去跳舞？(看書)

    →因為今天晚上我得看書。

1. 為什麼你不睡覺？(等我妹妹的電話)

2. 為什麼你不看電視？(練習說中文)

3. 為什麼你今天下午沒有空兒？(開會)

B. Answer the following questions.

1. 誰常常給你打電話？

2. 你是大學幾年級的學生？

3. 你星期四幾點鐘有中文課？

4. 你星期一有幾節課？

5. 你明天有沒有考試？

6. 你知道不知道你的中文老師叫什麼名字？

7. 你喜歡和同學一起去跳舞嗎？

C. Complete the following sentences with 但是.

1. 我想今天下午去找王老師，

   _____ 。

2. 我想這個週末去看電影，

   _____ 。

3. 我想請我的同學幫忙，

_____。

4. 我想給你打電話，

_____。

D. Rearrange the following Chinese words into sentences, using the English sentences as clues.

1. 四點/我/辦公室/電話/在/明天/等/以後/下
午/你的

(I will be waiting for your phone call in the office after 4:00 p.m. tomorrow.)

2. 有人/不知道/請我/晚上/回來/什麼/時候/今
天/吃晚飯

(Someone is taking me out for dinner this evening. I don't know when I will
be back.)

3. 您/回來/給我/方便/請/以後/打/要是/電話

(If it is convenient for you, please give me a call after you come back.)

Translation

Translate the following sentences into Chinese, using the words or phrases in
parentheses.

1. Because I need to take a Chinese exam next Thursday, I'd like to ask Wang
Peng to help me practice speaking Chinese this weekend.
(因為...所以，請，幫)

2. I'll wait for you, but you have to treat me to a movie. (但是，得)

3. I'll go look for you after I get back. (以後)

4. I'll wait for your call after I get back home. (以後，等)

5. Sorry! I will not be free next week.

Writing Practice

A. Write a note to your Chinese friend to see if he/she can practice Chinese with you tomorrow evening. Promise him/her that you will buy him/her a cup of coffee afterwards.

B. Write a description of Little Wang's life.

Little Wang is often busy. He likes to go to the movies, but he has no time for that; he also likes to listen to music, but he has no time for that, either. Tomorrow he will be free. He will take Miss Bai out to dinner tomorrow evening. He doesn't know when she will be back home tomorrow afternoon, but he will wait for her to call.

LESSON 7 ▲ Studying Chinese
第七課 ▲ 學中文
Dì qī kè ▲ Xué Zhōngwén

Part One

DIALOGUE I: ASKING ABOUT AN EXAMINATION

I. Listening Comprehension

A. Textbook Dialogue I (True/False)

Quote the key sentence from the dialogue to support your answer.

( ) 1. Li You didn't do very well on her test last week.

( ) 2. Wang Peng writes Chinese well, but very slowly.

( ) 3. Wang Peng didn't want to teach Li You how to write Chinese characters.

( ) 4. Li You is prepared for tomorrow's lesson.

( ) 5. The Chinese characters in Lesson Seven are very easy.

( ) 6. Li You has no problems with Lesson Seven's grammar.

B. Workbook Narrative (True/False)

Quote the key sentence from the dialogue to support your answer.

( ) 1. Mr. Li is an American.

( ) 2. Mr. Li likes studying Chinese, but not English.

( ) 3. Mr. Li feels that English grammar is not too difficult, but Chinese grammar is hard.

( ) 4. Mr. Li is having a hard time learning Chinese characters.

C. Workbook Dialogue I (True/False)

(Little Wang is talking to Little Bai.)

( ) 1. Little Bai didn't do very well on the Chinese test last week.

( ) 2. Little Wang is not willing to practice Chinese with Little Bai.

(   ) 3. Little Bai is very good at Chinese characters.

(   ) 4. Little Wang can help Little Bai with both speaking and writing.

II. Speaking Exercises

A. Answer the questions in Chinese based on Textbook Dialogue I.

1. How did Li You do on last week's test, and why?

2. Why does Wang Peng offer to help Li You with her writing of Chinese characters?

3. Who can write Chinese characters fast?

4. Which lesson will Li You study tomorrow?

5. How does Li You feel about the grammar, vocabulary and characters in the lesson she has prepared?

6. What will Wang Peng and Li You do tonight?

B. Discuss the results of the recent Chinese tests you have taken with your friend. Comment on how you did on grammar, vocabulary and Chinese characters.

C. Make up a story based on the picture below. Try to use the new words and sentence structures that you have learned in this lesson.

▼▼▼▼▼▼▼▼▼▼▼▼▼▼▼▼▼▼▼▼▼▼▼▼▼▼▼▼▼▼▼▼▼▼

III. Reading Comprehension

A. Read the note and answer the questions. (True/False)

小王：

　你好！我上個星期有個中文考試，我考得不太好，老師說我漢字寫得不錯，可是太慢。中文語法也有一點兒難，我不太懂。這個週末你有時間嗎？我想請你幫助我復習中文。我們一起練習說中文，好嗎？

　　　　　　　　小白

　　　　　　　　十月二十七日

Questions:

（　）1. 小白上個星期考試考得不錯。

（　）2. 老師說小白寫漢字寫得很好，也很快。

（　）3. 小白覺得中文語法很容易，她都懂。

（　）4. 小白要小王幫助她復習中文。

B. Read the passage and answer the questions. (True/False)

昨天是小高的生日，李友和王朋都到小高家去了。他們一起喝啤酒，聽音樂，唱歌，晚上十二點才回家，一點鐘才睡覺。因為李友沒有復習中文，所以今天考試考得不好。

Questions:

( ) 1. 李友和王朋都是小高的朋友。

( ) 2. 昨天晚上十點鐘李友、王朋和小高都不在家。

( ) 3. 王朋昨天晚上喝啤酒了，可是李友沒有喝。

( ) 4. 李友昨天沒有時間復習中文。

( ) 5. 王朋昨天晚上睡覺睡得很晚。

( ) 6. 李友覺得今天的考試很容易。

IV. Writing & Grammar Exercises

Grammar and Usage

A. Answer the following questions.

Example: A: 你昨天睡覺睡得晚嗎？

B: 我睡覺睡得很晚。

1. A: 你寫字寫得快嗎？

B: _____ 。

2. A: 你妹妹唱歌唱得好嗎？

B: _____ 。

3. A: 你哥哥打球打得好嗎？

B: _____ 。

4. A: 她跳舞跳得怎麼樣？

B: _____ 。

5. A: 你說中文說得怎麼樣？

B: _____ 。

B. Fill in the blanks based on the hints given in parentheses.

我和我的姐姐 _____ (both) 喜歡聽 _____ (music)。我們 _____ (often) _____ (together) 聽。我們 _____ (also) 喜歡 _____ (study) 中文。_____ (however)，中國人說中文說得 _____ (too) 快。我 _____ (feel) 語法也 _____ (a bit) 難。

C. Complete the sentences with 才 *or* 就:

Example: 我們三點開會，可是<u>李小姐四點才來</u>。(才)

我們三點開會，可是<u>李小姐兩點就來了</u>。(就)

1. 我們八點鐘有中文課，可是

　　_____。(才)

2. 小王今天下午沒有課，所以

　　_____。(就)

3. 我昨天晚上去朋友家玩兒，

　　_____。(才)

4. 她媽媽說明天來，可是

　　_____。(就)

5. 因為我今天有考試，所以我昨天晚上復習生詞，

　　_____。(才)

6. 我哥哥說今天晚上給我打電話，可是

　　_____。(就)

D. Make sentences using the given words and 得.

Example: 說中文/好

→ 他說中文說得很好。

1. 寫字/好

2. 說英文/快

3. 打球/不好

4. 學漢字/不太快

5. 喝啤酒/多

Translation

Translate the following sentences into Chinese, using the words or phrases in parentheses.

1. The teacher writes Chinese characters very well.

2. She feels that Chinese grammar is a little bit hard. (有一點兒)

3. Because I am very busy, I will not go to the library until tomorrow afternoon. (就/才)

4. I went to the school (as early as) at seven o'clock today.

5. You write characters too slowly. (太... 了)

6. I feel that the text of Lesson Six is a little difficult.

7. Teach me how to write Chinese characters, OK?

8. Please help me review Lesson Six, OK?

Writing Practice

Write a paragraph (5–10 sentences) describing your experience learning Chinese.

Part Two

DIALOGUE II: PREPARING FOR A CHINESE CLASS

I. Listening Comprehension

A. Textbook Dialogue II (True/False)

Quote the key sentence from the dialogue to support your answer.

( ) 1. Little Bai is always late.

( ) 2. Little Bai didn't go to bed until after midnight last night.

( ) 3. Li You went to bed very late, because she was studying Chinese.

( ) 4. Little Bai has a very good Chinese friend.

( ) 5. Li You recited the lesson well, because she listened to the recording the night before.

( ) 6. Li You has a very handsome Chinese friend according to Little Bai.

B. Workbook Dialogue II (True/False)

Quote the key sentence from the dialogue to support your answer.

(Little Li is talking to Little Zhang.)

( ) 1. Little Zhang usually comes early.

( ) 2. Little Zhang previewed Lesson Eight.

( ) 3. Little Zhang went to bed early because he didn't have homework last night.

( ) 4. Little Zhang usually goes to bed around 9:00 p.m.

II. Speaking Exercises

A. Answer the questions in Chinese based on Textbook Dialogue II.

1. Why did Little Bai come so late today?

2. Why was Li You able to go to bed early last night?

3. Why did Little Bai say that it is nice to have a Chinese friend?

4. Which lesson is the class studying today?

5. Who did not listen to the recording last night?

6. How did Little Bai describe Li You's friend?

B. Find out why your friend is late or early for the class, and how he/she prepares for each new lesson.

III. Reading Comprehension

A. Read Li You's schedule for today and answer the questions. (True/False)

上午	八點半	預習生詞
	九點一刻	聽錄音
	十點	上中文課
中午	十二點	吃午飯
下午	一點	睡午覺
	兩點	復習中文
晚上	六點	吃晚飯
	八點	做功課

Questions:

( ) 1. 李友今天沒有課。

( ) 2. 李友上午預習生詞。

( ) 3. 李友下午聽錄音。

( ) 4. 李友不吃午飯，只吃晚飯。

( ) 5. 李友復習中文以後睡午覺。

( ) 6. 李友吃晚飯以後做功課。

B. Read the passage and answer the questions. (True/False)

今天上午，小李預習了第六課。第六課的語法有點兒難，生詞也很多。下午她要去老師的辦公室問問題。她覺得學中文很有意思。說中國話不太難，可是漢字有一點兒難。

Questions:

（　）1. 小李覺得第六課不太容易。

（　）2. 今天下午小李的老師在辦公室。

（　）3. 小李想今天下午給老師打電話。

（　）4. 小李很喜歡學中文。

（　）5. 小李覺得學漢字不容易。

IV. Writing & Grammar Exercises

Grammar and Usage

A. Complete the sentences or fill in sentences in the dialogues using 因為 *or* 所以.

1. 因為昨天晚上沒有功課，

   ＿＿＿＿＿＿＿＿＿＿＿＿＿＿＿＿＿＿＿＿＿。

2. 因為你有中國朋友幫助你復習，

   ＿＿＿＿＿＿＿＿＿＿＿＿＿＿＿＿＿＿＿＿＿。

3. A: 你怎麼沒去看電影？

   B: ＿＿＿＿＿＿＿＿＿＿＿＿＿＿＿＿＿＿＿。

4. A: 你為什麼請他喝咖啡？

   B: ＿＿＿＿＿＿＿＿＿＿＿＿＿＿＿＿＿＿＿。

5. ＿＿＿＿＿＿＿＿＿＿＿＿＿＿＿＿＿＿＿＿＿，

   所以他很晚才睡覺。

B. Fill in the blanks with 真 *or* 太.

1. 你這張照片 ＿＿＿＿＿＿ 漂亮。
2. 那個學校 ＿＿＿＿＿＿ 大了。
3. 今天的功課 ＿＿＿＿＿＿ 多了。
4. 這個工作 ＿＿＿＿＿＿ 有意思。
5. 第六課的生詞 ＿＿＿＿＿＿ 多。
6. 李友的媽媽 ＿＿＿＿＿＿ 客氣了。

Translation

Translate the following sentences into Chinese, using the words or phrases in parentheses.

1. Last night I was not back home until ten o'clock. (就/才)

2. How come your younger brother didn't go to the movie on Wednesday?

3. His older sister sings really well. (真)

4. *A:* How come you are so happy today? (怎麼)

   B: Because I did very well on the test. (得)

5. I previewed Lesson Seven. The grammar is easy.

6. Your pen is really beautiful.

7. Good morning, everybody. Let's begin the lesson. Please read the text.

8. Your boyfriend is really handsome!

9. I listened to the tape. But I did not understand it.

Writing Practice

Translate the following paragraph into Chinese.

My younger sister did not learn Chinese well. She didn't like listening to recordings and didn't practice speaking, so she did not speak well. She didn't like studying grammar or writing characters. That was why she didn't do well on examinations. But after she met a Chinese friend, she and her friend often practice speaking Chinese in the library. Now, she likes listening to tapes and writing characters.

LESSON 8 ▲ School Life
第八課 ▲ 學校生活
Dì bā kè ▲ *Xuéxiào shēnghuó*

Part One

A DIARY: A TYPICAL SCHOOL DAY

I. Listening Comprehension

A. A Diary (Multiple Choice)

(   ) 1. Which day of the week is August 10?

    a. Monday   b. Tuesday   c. Wednesday   d. Thursday

(   ) 2. What did Li You do this morning before breakfast?

    a. She took a bath.

    b. She listened to the recording.

    c. She read the newspaper.

    d. She talked to her friend on the phone.

(   ) 3. What time did Li You go to class this morning?

    a. 7:30   b. 8:00   c. 8:30   d. 9:00

(   ) 4. What did Li You NOT do in her Chinese class?

    a. take a test   b. practice pronunciation

    c. learn vocabulary   d. study grammar

(   ) 5. Where did Li You have lunch today?

    a. at a Chinese restaurant   b. in the school's dining hall

    c. at home   d. at her friend's house

(   ) 6. What was Li You doing around 4:30 p.m.?

    a. practicing Chinese   b. reading a newspaper

    c. playing ball   d. drinking coffee

(   ) 7. What time did Li You eat her dinner?

    a. 5:45   b. 6:00   c. 6:30   d. 7:30

( ) 8. Li You went to Little Bai's dorm to:

    a. eat dinner.   b. read the newspaper.

    c. chat.   d. study.

( ) 9. What time did Li You return home?

    a. 7:30   b. 8:30   c. 9:30   d. 10:30

( ) 10. What did Li You do before she went to bed?

    a. visited Little Bai   b. did her homework

    c. called Wang Peng   d. prepared for her test

B. Use the numbers 1-3 to put the pictures in the correct sequence based on the information given in A Diary.

    ( )   ( )   ( )

C. Workbook Dialogue (True/False)

Quote the key sentence from the dialogue to support your answer.

( ) 1. Li You is going to Teacher Zhang's office at 4:00 p.m. today.

( ) 2. Wang Peng will be attending a class at 2:30 p.m. today.

( ) 3. Li You plans to read newspapers in the library this evening.

( ) 4. Li You and Wang Peng will see each other in the library this evening.

II. Speaking Exercises

A. Answer the questions in Chinese based on A Diary.

1. When was the diary entry written?

2. What time did Li You get up on that day?

3. What did Li You do before 9:00 a.m. on that day?

4. What did Li You do in her Chinese class on that day?

5. Did Li You like her computer class? Why?

6. What did Li You do during the lunch hour?

7. What did Li You do that afternoon?

8. Describe what Li You did that evening.

B. *Call your Chinese friend and describe to him/her what you did yesterday at school.*

C. *Tell a story based on the pictures below. Don't forget to mention the times.*

III. Reading Comprehension

A. *Answer the questions about* A Diary *in English or in Chinese.*

1. 這是幾月幾號的日記？

2. 李友早上開始聽錄音以前做什麼事？

3. 今天上午李友有幾節課？是什麼課？

4. 李友中午在哪兒吃飯？

5. 李友下午在圖書館做什麼？

6. 李友跟誰一起打球？

7. 李友為什麼去找小白？

8. 李友告訴王朋什麼事？

B. *Read the following schedule and answer the questions. (True/False)*

<table>
<tr><td colspan="2" align="center">小張今天要做的事：</td></tr>
<tr><td>8:00</td><td>復習第七課生詞、語法</td></tr>
<tr><td>9:00</td><td>上電腦課</td></tr>
<tr><td>10:00</td><td>去王老師辦公室練習發音</td></tr>
<tr><td>14:30</td><td>去圖書館看報</td></tr>
<tr><td>16:00</td><td>去打球</td></tr>
<tr><td>18:00</td><td>去宿舍餐廳吃飯</td></tr>
<tr><td>20:15</td><td>給小李打電話，請他一起練習中文</td></tr>
<tr><td>21:30</td><td>給爸爸媽媽打電話</td></tr>
</table>

Questions:

( )1. 小張今天只有一節課。

( )2. 小張跟小白一起吃午飯。

( )3. 小張上午去見王老師。

( )4. 小張去小李家練習中文。

( )5. 小張吃晚飯以前去打球。

( )6. 小張去圖書館以後去找王老師。

( )7. 小張睡覺以前給爸爸媽媽打電話。

( )8. 小張練習中文以後才吃飯。

C. Read the passage and answer the questions. (True/False)

小白以前常常跟朋友一起打球，聊天，看電視，不做功課。可是因為他下星期要考試，所以這個星期他不打球，不看電視，也不找朋友聊天，一個人到圖書館去看書。他很早就起床，很晚才睡覺，所以他上課的時候常常想睡覺。

Questions:

( )1. 小白以前常常跟朋友一邊做功課，一邊聊天。

( )2. 小白常常跟朋友到圖書館去看書。

( )3. 小白這個星期不打球，也不看電視，可是找朋友聊天兒。

( ) 4. 小白覺得上課沒有意思，所以他上課
的時候常常想睡覺。

( ) 5. 這個星期小白睡覺睡得很早。

IV. Writing & Grammar Exercises

Grammar and Usage

A. Complete the following dialogues. Each sentence should contain a double-object structure.

Example: A: 他教<u>誰</u>中文？

→ 他教<u>他弟弟中文</u>。

1. A: 王老師教學生_____？
   B: 王老師教_____。

2. A: 小高給_____一本書？
   B: 小高給_____。

3. A: 李友問誰_____？
   B: 李友問_____。

4. A: 高小音給_____一杯茶？
   B: 高小音給_____。

5. A: 你告訴王朋_____了？
   B: 我告訴王朋_____。

▼▼▼▼▼▼▼▼▼▼▼▼▼▼▼▼▼▼▼▼▼▼▼▼▼▼▼▼▼▼▼▼▼▼▼▼▼

B. Follow the model and rewrite the sentences.

Example: 他吃飯的時候聽音樂。

→ 他一邊吃飯一邊聽音樂。

1. 他聽音樂的時候看報。

2. 我們吃飯的時候練習說中文。

3. 我的朋友喜歡寫字的時候聽音樂。

4. 張小姐吃飯的時候看電視。

Translation

Translate the following sentences into Chinese, using the words or phrases in parentheses.

1. My older sister taught me to sing, and I taught her to dance.

2. She wrote her Chinese diary very well. (complement with 得)

3. A: I'd like to go to the dining hall to have lunch. (到...去 + v)

B: I had lunch as early as eleven. (就) I want to go to the library to read the newspapers. (到...去 + V)

4. My older brother takes a shower right after getting up. (以後，就)

5. Li You dances very well, but she does not dance much. (complement with 得，不常)

6. I go to class after breakfast. (以後)

7. When I went to Little Li's dorm yesterday morning, she was chatting with Little Bai. (...的時候，...正在...)

8. I told my teacher already.

Writing Practice

Write a diary entry in Chinese about your school life.

▼ ▼

Part Two

A LETTER: TALKING ABOUT STUDYING CHINESE

I. Listening Comprehension

A. A Letter (True/False)

Quote the key sentence from the dialogue to support your answer.

( ) 1. This is a letter from Yiwen to Miss Zhang.

( ) 2. Yiwen's major is Chinese.

( ) 3. Yiwen does not like her Chinese class at all.

( ) 4. Yiwen's Chinese friend speaks very clearly.

( ) 5. Yiwen is learning Chinese fast, because she has a Chinese friend.

( ) 6. Yiwen would like Miss Zhang to attend her school concert.

B. Workbook Narrative

( ) 1. Wang Peng went to the library to help Li You with her Chinese.

( ) 2. Wang Peng did not go to play ball this afternoon until he had finished his homework.

( ) 3. Li You went to a movie with Wang Peng this evening.

( ) 4. Li You has a Chinese class tomorrow.

II. Speaking Exercises

A. Answer the questions in Chinese based on A Letter.

1. Why is Yiwen so busy this semester?

2. Describe Yiwen's Chinese class.

3. Is Yiwen making progress in her Chinese class? Why?

4. Why did Yiwen ask Miss Zhang if she likes music?

5. Do you think Yiwen has confidence in her Chinese? Why?

B. Describe your Chinese class in detail to your friend. Make sure to comment on how you feel about pronunciation, grammar, vocabulary, and Chinese characters.

▼▼▼▼▼▼▼▼▼▼▼▼▼▼▼▼▼▼▼▼▼▼▼▼▼▼▼▼▼▼▼▼▼▼▼▼

C. *Interview your classmate and find out:*

    1. when he/she gets up in the morning;

    2. whether he/she takes a shower in the morning after getting up or before going to bed at night;

    3. whether he/she prefers to have lunch at home or at school;

    4. what time he/she goes to school;

    5. what time he/she has his/her lunches and dinners;

    6. what time he/she returns home after school;

    7. what time he/she goes to bed.

III. Reading Comprehension

A. *Answer the questions about* A Letter.

1. 寫信的人叫什麼名字？

2. 你覺得意文喜歡她的中文課嗎？為什麼？

3. 上中文課的時候意文能說英文嗎？

4. 意文常常跟誰一起練習說中文？

5. 意文為什麼給張小姐寫信？

▼ ▼

B. Read the note and answer the questions. (True/False)

小王：

今天晚上七點半學校有一個很好的音樂會，我想請你跟我一起去。請你回來以後給我打電話。我的電話是：八五七九五六三。

小謝

七月五日下午四點半

Questions:

( ) 1. Little Xie plans to call Little Wang this evening at 7:30.

( ) 2. At 4:30 Little Wang was most likely not home.

( ) 3. Little Xie is certain that Little Wang knows her phone number.

( ) 4. Little Xie is hoping to spend the evening with Little Wang.

C. Read the passage and answer the questions. (True/False)

小張今天很忙，上午除了有三節課以外，還有一個電腦考試。中午跟朋友一起吃飯，下午在圖書館看書，做功課，晚上在電腦室工作，十點鐘回家吃晚飯。晚飯以後，他一邊看電視，一邊預習明天的功課，十二點半才睡覺。

Questions:

( ) 1. 小張上午沒空。

( )2. 小張下午不在家，在圖書館看報。

( )3. 小張晚上很晚才吃飯。

( )4. 小張晚上在電腦室預習明天的功課。

( )5. 小張一邊聽音樂，一邊看書。

IV. Writing & Grammar Exercises

Grammar and Usage

A.. *Following the model, combine the sentences in each group into one that contains the* "除了...以外，還" *structure.*

Example: 我學中文。我也學日文。

→除了中文以外，我還學日文。

1. 我喜歡聽音樂。我也喜歡跳舞。

2. 他常常打球。他也常常看電影。

3. 今天晚上我想寫信。今天晚上我也想給我媽媽打電話。

4. 明天我有一節電腦課。明天我也有兩節英文課。

5. 他預習了生詞。他也預習了課文。

6. 我喜歡打球。我也喜歡找朋友聊天。

B. *Answer the questions.*

1. 除了中文課以外，你還有什麼課？

2. 你常常跟誰一起去看電影？

3. 你平常睡覺以前做什麼？

4. 你平常起床以後做什麼？

Translation

Translate the following sentences into Chinese, using the words or phrases in parentheses.

1. At the beginning, I was not used to listening to the recording while having breakfast at the same time.

2. This morning the teacher gave us a lot of homework.

3. I hope that you can go to the concert with me.

▼▼

4. We often speak Chinese and play ball at the same time. (一邊…一邊…)

5. In addition to pronunciation, Mr. Wang also teaches us grammar. (除了…以外，也…)

6. Wang Peng read the text very well. (complement with 得)

7. She made a lot of progress with her pronunciation.

8. In the beginning, he didn't speak Chinese clearly.

9. Do not laugh at other people.

10. I hope you will make a lot of progress with your Chinese.

11. Previously, she told me that her major was computers.

12. When I went to see her, she was writing a letter to her boyfriend. (…的時候，…正在…)

Writing Practice

Write your friend a letter in Chinese telling him/her about your experience learning Chinese.

Example:

My Chinese class is hard, but I think it is pretty interesting. My Chinese friend often helps me, and that is the reason my Chinese has improved rapidly. In addition to practicing speaking Chinese, I also play ball and go to movies with my friend. Both my friend and I are happy.

LESSON 9 ▲ Shopping
第九課 ▲ 買東西
Dì jiǔ kè ▲ *Mǎi dōngxi*

Part One

DIALOGUE I: BUYING CLOTHING

I. Listening Comprehension

A. Textbook Dialogue I (Multiple Choice)

( ) 1. What color shirt does the customer want to buy?

    a. black   b. white   c. red   d. yellow

( ) 2. What else does the customer want to buy besides the shirt?

    a. a hat   b. a pair of shoes

    c. a sweater   d. a pair of pants

( ) 3. What size does the customer wear?

    a. small   b. medium   c. large   d. extra large

( ) 4. How much does the customer need to pay altogether?

    a. between $20 and $30   b. between $30 and $40

    c. between $40 and $50   d. between $50 and $60

B. Workbook Narrative (Multiple Choice)

( ) 1. What color does Wang Peng like?

    a. blue   b. brown   c. white   d. red

( ) 2. Why does Wang Peng not like the shirt? Because of the:

    a. price   b. style   c. color   d. size

( ) 3. What colors are the shirts that the salesperson says they have?

    a. white, blue, and brown   b. white, red, and brown

    c. red, blue, and white   d. white, red, and yellow

( ) 4. When did Wang Peng buy the shirt?

    a. 5 days ago   b. 7 days ago   c. 10 days ago   d. 14 days ago

II. Speaking Exercises

A. Answer the questions in Chinese based on Textbook Dialogue I.

1. What does the woman want to buy?

2. Is the woman very rich? How do you know?

3. Give the price for each item, and the total cost.

4. If the woman gives the salesperson $100, how much change should she receive?

B. You are in a department store, trying to buy a shirt and a pair of pants. Tell the salesperson what color and size you want.

C. Describe the four pictures below without looking at the textbook.

III. Reading Comprehension

A. Answer the questions about Textbook Dialogue I.

1. 李小姐買了一件什麼顏色的襯衫？

2. 她買了一條多大的褲子？

3. 襯衫一件多少錢？褲子一條多少錢？

4. 售貨員找了多少錢給李小姐？

B. Read the following passage and answer the questions. (True/False)

小高上個週末去買東西。他想買一件中號的紅襯衫，可是中號襯衫都是白的，紅襯衫都是大號的。售貨員是一位很客氣的小姐。她幫小高找了一件襯衫，不是紅的，可是顏色也不錯。那位售貨員告訴他，這件襯衫三十九塊九毛九。小高覺得太貴了一點兒，可是他覺得要是不買就對不起那位小姐，所以他買了那件襯衫。

Questions:

(　　) 1. There were many choices in the store for Xiao Gao to select from.

(　　) 2. The saleswoman was very helpful.

(　　) 3. Last weekend Xiao Gao was looking for a white shirt.

(　　) 4. Xiao Gao bought the shirt because he thought he shouldn't disappoint the saleswoman.

(　　) 5. Xiao Gao wears a medium size shirt.

▼ ▼

IV. Writing & Grammar Exercises

Grammar and Usage

Give Chinese characters for the following dollar amounts.

1. $5.12 _____
2. $18.50 _____
3. $70.05 _____
4. $99.99 _____
5. $100.60 _____

Translation

Translate the following sentences into Chinese, using the words or phrases in parentheses.

1. Would you like to watch TV or listen to music? (想，還是)

2. That large-size shirt is my older brother's, and this small-size one is mine. (的)

3. The yellow shirts are expensive, and the white ones are cheap. (Adj. + 的)

4. The medium red shirt is $8.95. Your change is one dollar.

5. The new words in Lesson Nine are not too many, and not too few, either.

6. A bottle of beer is $3.00 and a glass of cola is 75¢. (That's) $3.75 altogether.

7. The salesperson asked what he would like to buy.

8. You pay here. It's $436.72 altogether.

9. What size do you wear? (多大)

Writing Practice

A. Write a shopping list in Chinese, including the names and prices of the items you want to purchase.

B. *Describe what you are wearing in Chinese. Don't forget to mention color and size.*

▼▼▼

Part Two

DIALOGUE II: EXCHANGING SHOES

I. Listening Comprehension

A. Textbook Dialogue II (True/False)

Quote the key sentence from the dialogue to support your answer.

( ) 1. Why does the lady want to exchange the shoes?

a. The shoes do not fit well.

b. The shoes are damaged.

c. She does not like the price.

d. She does not like the color.

( ) 2. What color does the lady prefer?

a. black   b. white   c. brown   d. red

( ) 3. In what way are the new pair of shoes like the old pair? They are:

a. the same size.   b. the same color.

c. the same price.   d. the same design.

B. Workbook Dialogue (True/False)

Quote the key sentence from the dialogue to support your answer.

( ) 1. The man returned his shirt for a different one, because he didn't like the color.

( ) 2. The man finally took a yellow shirt because he liked the color.

( ) 3. All the large-size shirts in the store are yellow ones.

( ) 4. A large-size shirt fits the man well.

II. Speaking Exercises

A. Answer the questions in Chinese based on Textbook Dialogue II.

1. Why did the woman want to return the shoes for a different pair?

2. Does the woman like black shoes? Explain.

3. What color of shoes did she finally accept? Why?

4. Did the woman pay any additional money for the new shoes? Explain.

B. You bought a shirt that is too large. Try to exchange it for a smaller one.

C. Describe the clothes you are wearing today.

III. Reading Comprehension

A. Answer the questions about Textbook Dialogue II.

1. 李小姐為什麼想換鞋？

2. 李小姐想換什麼顏色的鞋？

3. 李小姐換了鞋沒有？ 她換了一雙什麼鞋？

B. Read the passage and answer the questions.

上星期六，小張買了一條褲子。她想買黑色的，可是只有黃的和紅的，她買了一條紅的。回家以後，覺得不太喜歡那條褲子的顏色，想明天下午去換一條別的顏色的褲子。

Questions:

1. 上星期六小張買了什麼顏色的褲子？

2.小張喜歡什麼顏色的褲子？

3.小張為什麼不喜歡她的新褲子？

4.明天下午小張要做什麼？

C. *Read the passage and answer the questions (True/False).*

李太太很喜歡買東西，最喜歡買便宜的衣服。雖然她的衣服很多，可是都不太合適。李先生跟他太太不一樣，不喜歡買東西，也不常買東西。李先生只買大小合適的衣服，所以，李先生的衣服雖然不多，可是都很合適。

Questions:

( ) 1. 李太太覺得買東西很有意思。

( ) 2. 李太太的衣服很多，也都很貴。

( ) 3. 李太太的衣服大小和顏色都很合適。

( ) 4. 李先生覺得買衣服沒意思。

( ) 5. 李先生買了很多衣服。

( ) 6. 李先生的衣服不大也不小。

D. *Find the clothing items corresponding to the descriptions below. Place the correct letter in the parentheses next to its description.* [Note: This exercise contains supplementary vocabulary items.]

1. 短褲（　）   2. 長褲（　）   3. 大衣（　）

4. 帽子（　）   5. 襪子（　）   6. 裙子（　）

7. T-恤衫（　）   8. 西裝（　）   9. 夾克（　）

10. 外套（　）   11. 毛衣（　）

IV. Writing & Grammar Exercises

Grammar and Usage

A. *Fill in each of the blanks with an appropriate measure word.*

件，條，雙，本，瓶，位，節，封，篇，杯

1. 一 _____ 鞋   2. 一 _____ 襯衫

3. 兩 _____ 褲子   4. 三 _____ 課

5. 一 _____ 先生   6. 一 _____ 書

▼▼▼▼▼▼▼▼▼▼▼▼▼▼▼▼▼▼▼▼▼▼▼▼▼▼▼▼▼▼▼▼▼ ▼

7. 一 ＿＿＿＿＿ 日記　　8. 兩 ＿＿＿＿＿ 信

9. 一 ＿＿＿＿＿ 可樂　　10. 一 ＿＿＿＿＿ 茶

B. Complete the following sentences.

1. 這條褲子雖然顏色不太好，＿＿＿＿＿＿。
   (inexpensive)

2. 我雖然喜歡看電影，＿＿＿＿＿＿＿＿＿。(don't have time)

3. ＿＿＿＿＿＿＿＿(very difficult), 可是我很喜歡學。

4. 雖然他上個月才開始學中文，＿＿＿＿＿＿
   ＿＿＿＿＿＿＿。(speaks quite well)

5. ＿＿＿＿＿＿＿＿(I don't write well)，可是我很喜歡
   寫漢字。

C. Following the model, complete the following sentences using the pattern "A 跟 B 一樣 + Adj."

Example: 我的襯衫<u>跟我哥哥的襯衫一樣貴</u>。
         (貴)

1. 這雙鞋＿＿＿＿＿＿＿＿。(大)

2. 學英文＿＿＿＿＿＿＿＿。(有意思)

3. 我的褲子的顏色＿＿＿＿＿＿＿＿。(漂亮)

4. 你說中文＿＿＿＿＿＿＿＿。(快)

5. 第七課的功課＿＿＿＿＿＿＿＿。(難)

6. 學校餐廳的飯＿＿＿＿＿＿＿＿。(好吃)

D. Complete the following dialogue.

售貨員：＿＿＿＿＿＿＿＿＿？

李小姐：我想買一條褲子。

售貨員：＿＿＿＿＿＿＿＿＿？

李小姐：大號的。

售貨員：這條太大了，你可以換＿＿＿＿＿
　　　　＿＿＿＿＿。

李小姐：中號的很合適。

售貨員：＿＿＿＿＿＿＿＿＿？

李小姐：還要買一雙鞋。

售貨員：＿＿＿＿＿＿＿＿＿？

李小姐： 黃的。

售貨員： 一條褲子十九塊，一雙鞋十五

塊，一共 ＿＿＿＿＿＿＿＿＿＿＿＿。

李小姐： ＿＿＿＿＿＿＿＿＿＿＿＿。

售貨員： 找您六十六塊。

Translation

Translate the following sentences into Chinese, using the words or phrases in parentheses.

1. Do you want to buy a pair of black shoes or a pair of yellow ones?
(要，還是)

2. This pair of pants is just as expensive as that pair.

3. The color of your shirt is the same as mine.

4. Although this pair of shoes fits me well, I don't like the color. (雖然)

5. The brown shoes are not too expensive, but not too cheap, either.

6. You don't need to give me the change.

Writing Practice

Translate the following passage into Chinese.

Yesterday I bought a yellow shirt and a pair of black pants. The pants are very expensive, but the color is very nice and the size is right. Although the shirt is very pretty and also very cheap, it's too small. Tomorrow I'll exchange it for a large shirt.

LESSON 10 ▲ Talking about the Weather
第十課 ▲ 談天氣
Dì shí kè ▲ *Tán tiānqì*

Part One

DIALOGUE I: THE WEATHER IS GETTING BETTER

I. Listening Comprehension

A. Textbook Dialogue I (True/False)

Quote the key sentence from the dialogue to support your answer.

( ) 1. It rained yesterday.

( ) 2. The weather today is better than yesterday.

( ) 3. It will be warmer tomorrow than today.

( ) 4. Miss Li will go to see the red leaves tomorrow.

( ) 5. Mr. Wang went to Shanghai by himself.

( ) 6. The woman suggests that the man stay home tomorrow.

B. Workbook Dialogue I (Multiple Choice)

( ) 1. What season is it now?

    a. spring   b. summer   c. autumn   d. winter

( ) 2. Where was the woman this afternoon?

    a. in the classroom   b. in the park

    c. in the shopping mall   d. in the office

( ) 3. How will the weather be tomorrow?

    a. rainy   b. hot   c. sunny   d. warm

( ) 4. The man got the information on the weather from:

    a. the TV.   b. the newspaper.

    c. his friend.   d. the radio.

II. Speaking Exercises

A. Answer the questions in Chinese based on Textbook Dialogue I.

> 1. What did the weather forecast say about the weather tomorrow?
> 2. Was the man excited about the forecast of tomorrow's weather? Why?
> 3. Where will Miss Li most likely be tomorrow?
> 4. What did the woman suggest the man do tomorrow?

B. Compare two objects (books, pieces of clothing items, etc.) or two people (family members, friends, etc.).

C. Compare the two languages, Chinese and English.

III. Reading Comprehension

A. Answer the questions about Textbook Dialogue I.

1. 今天天氣怎麼樣？

2. 高先生明天想做什麼事？

3. 天氣預報說明天的天氣怎麼樣？

4. 高先生跟李小姐明天會去看紅葉嗎？為什麼？

B. Read the following passage and answer the questions. (True/False)

星期五下午王朋約了李友星期天一起去公園看紅葉。可是星期六報上的天氣預報說，星期天會下雨。王朋就給李友打了一個電話，告訴她星期天不去公園了。星期天上午王朋請李友來他的宿舍看錄像，可是星期天的天氣很好，不但沒下雨，而且很暖和。王朋說：「以後報上說會下雨，我們就可以去公園看紅葉。報上說天氣很好，我們就只能在家看錄像了。」

Questions:

( ) 1. The story took place in summer.

( ) 2. They had to change their plan for Sunday because of the weather forecast.

( ) 3. Wang Peng learned the weather forecast from the TV.

( ) 4. Wang Peng was glad that he and Li You were not out on Sunday.

( ) 5. Wang Peng thinks that the weather forecast is very reliable.

IV. Writing & Grammar Exercises

Grammar and Usage

A. Following the model, make sentences using the structure "不但...而且...".

Example: 漂亮 / 便宜

→ 這件襯衫不但很漂亮，而且很便宜。

1. 喜歡聽音樂/喜歡看錄像:

2. 常常下雨/冷:

3. 貴/顏色不好:

4. 不便宜/不合適:

5. 想去買東西/想去看紅葉:

B. Complete the sentences and expand the dialogue.

A: 小謝，明天是星期六，我們去公園看紅葉，

_____？

B: 好啊，可是我聽天氣預報說

_____。

A: 那我們星期天再去吧。

B: 可是下個星期天的天氣

_____ 。

A: 那怎麼辦呢？

B: _____ 。

Translation

Translate the following sentences into Chinese, using the words or phrases in parentheses.

1. We can not only speak Chinese but also write letters in Chinese.
   (不但...而且...)

2. English is difficult, but Japanese is more difficult. (更)

3. The weather forecast in the newspaper says that the weather will be better next week. (會)

▼ ▼

4. Eating Chinese food is more convenient than eating American food.
   (比)

5. The black shoes are more expensive than the red ones. (比)

6. I would like to make a date with Miss Li to go to the park to see the red leaves.

7. Watching a video is cheaper than going to the movies.

Writing Practice

Write a paragraph comparing two things or people. Be sure to use these expressions: 不但...而且..., *and* 比.

▼▼▼

Part Two

DIALOGUE: COMPLAINING ABOUT THE WEATHER

I. Listening Comprehension

A. Textbook Dialogue II (True/False)

Quote the key sentence from the dialogue to support your answer.

( ) 1. It has been raining often recently.

( ) 2. The weather will be better next week.

( ) 3. This weekend is not a good time to go out, for it is going to be cold and wet.

( ) 4. It will be hotter in two months.

( ) 5. Little Ye is in Taiwan for a visit.

( ) 6. The best time to visit Taiwan is in the spring.

B. Workbook Dialogue II (True/False)

Quote the key sentence from the dialogue to support your answer.

( ) 1. Wang Peng had an outing with Li You today.

( ) 2. Wang Peng does not like the weather because it started to rain in the morning.

( ) 3. The weather forecast says that the weather will be somewhat better tomorrow.

( ) 4. Tomorrow Wang Peng will be preparing his lessons for Monday.

( ) 5. Wang Peng believes that next Saturday it will be even cooler than tomorrow.

( ) 6. The dialogue most likely occurred on a Sunday.

II. Speaking Exercises

A. Answer the questions in Chinese based on Textbook Dialogue II.

1. What did the newspaper say about the weather this week and next week?

2. Why couldn't they go out to have fun this weekend?

3. Describe Taiwan's weather.

4. Why is Little Xia not very familiar with the weather in Taiwan?

B. Describe the climate of your hometown.

C. Compare the weather of your hometown with the weather of another place.

III. Reading Comprehension

A. Answer the questions about Textbook Dialogue II.

1. 小夏怎麼知道這個星期的天氣都不好？

2. 台北夏天的天氣很舒服，對不對？

3. 小葉住 (zhù: to live) 在哪兒？

4. 台灣什麼時候天氣最好？

B. Read the passage and answer the questions. (True/False)

黃先生以前住 (zhù: to live) 在台中，台中的天氣很好，常常不冷不熱，很舒服。黃先生現在在台北工作。台北的冬天天氣很糟糕，不但很冷，而且常常下雨。他看報上的天氣預報說這個週末台北會下雨，可是台中的天氣很好，他想約夏小姐星期天到台中去玩。

Questions:

（　）1. 黃先生現在不住在台中了。

（　）2. 台中的天氣很不錯。

（　）3. 台北的冬天雖然常常下雨，可是很暖和。

（　）4. 這個週末台北的天氣比台中好。

（　）5. 黃先生聽朋友說這個週末台北會下雨。

（　）6. 夏小姐住在台中。

C. Read the passage and answer the questions. (True/False)

[Note: See the supplementary vocabulary list for the new words.]

葉小姐一個人在加拿大的溫哥華工作，她的爸爸媽媽住在香港。葉小姐常常去看她的爸爸媽媽，可是她不喜歡夏天回香港，因為香港的夏天又悶又熱。葉小姐想請她爸爸媽媽到溫哥華來住。可是她的爸爸媽媽已經習慣了香港的天氣，而且他們在加拿大沒有朋友，所以他們覺得住在那兒沒有意思。

Questions:

（　）1. 葉小姐的爸爸媽媽常常來加拿大。

（　）2. 葉小姐常常在夏天回香港。

（　）3. 葉小姐的爸爸媽媽不覺得香港的夏天太熱。

( ) 4. 葉小姐的爸爸媽媽在溫哥華沒有朋
友。

( ) 5. 葉小姐覺得溫哥華夏天的天氣比香港
好。

( ) 6. 葉小姐的爸爸媽媽覺得住在香港比住
在溫哥華有意思。

D. *Read the following dialogue and answer the questions. (True/False)*

（老王和老李打電話聊天。）

老王：要是我下個月工作不忙，我想去台
北玩兒。

老李：你最好秋天來，下個月這兒天氣太
熱了。九月以後會涼快一點兒。

老王：台北的冬天怎麼樣？

老李：冬天？冬天比夏天更糟糕，不但
冷，而且常常下雨。

老王：是嗎？那我們這兒的天氣比你們那
兒好，不冷也不熱。

老李：真的啊？那太舒服了！

Questions:

( ) 1. Most likely the telephone conversation took place in September.

( ) 2. Lao Li lives in Taipei.

( ) 3. According to Lao Li, the best season to visit Taipei is autumn.

( ) 4. In comparison with summer, winter in Taipei is a little better.

( ) 5. Winter in Taipei is dry, not cold.

IV. Writing & Grammar Exercises

Grammar and Usage

A. Choose the appropriate adverbs to fill in the blanks. (真，太，又，再，更，很)

1. 今天的天氣 _____ 熱了。

2. 這個錄像 _____ 好看，我要 _____ 看
   一次。

3. 這件衣服 _____ 便宜 _____ 好看。

4. 上個星期的天氣不好，這個星期的天氣
   _____ 糟糕。

5. 我覺得寫中國字 _____ 有意思。

6. 他喜歡看電視，但是他 _____ 喜歡打
   球。

7. 他昨天給他弟弟打了一個電話，今天
   _____ 給他打了一個電話。

8. 這兒 _____ 有意思，我們下個月 _____
   來一次，好嗎？

9. 昨天晚上他不在家，我想他 _____ 去看
   電影了。

10. 第五課的生詞 _____ 多，可是第六課的
    生詞 _____ 多。

B. *Rewrite the sentences in each group into one sentence that expresses a comparison with the word* 比.

    Example: 昨天的天氣熱。今天的天氣不太熱。

       → 今天的天氣比昨天涼快。

      or: 昨天的天氣比今天熱。

1. 他這個星期很忙。他上個星期不太忙。

2. 中文很難，日文更難。

3. 這本書貴。那本書更貴。

4. 台灣的春天不舒服，秋天舒服。

5. 這兒的天氣很暖和。那兒的天氣更暖和。

C. *Write a sentence for each of the situations given below.*

    Example: Today's temperatures: Shanghai, ninety-five degrees; Beijing, seventy-five degrees.

      → 今天上海比北京熱。

      or: 今天北京比上海涼快。

1. Today's temperatures: Hong Kong, ninety degrees; Shanghai, eighty-five degrees.

▼ ▼

2. Prices for the shirts: yellow ones, $16 each; white ones, $18 each.

3. Mr. Wang is 5'8"; Mr. Wang's son is 6'2."

4. Little Bai has five books; Little Li has eight books.

5. Chinese is hard; Japanese is harder.

6. Lawyer Zhang is very polite; Lawyer Gao is not too polite.

7. The yellow shirt is not that pretty; the red shirt is very pretty.

8. Beer is expensive; cola is not that expensive.

9. Watching TV is not very interesting; going to the movies is really fun.

10. My father's office is big; my mother's office is not that big.

Translation

Translate the following sentences into Chinese, using the words or phrases in parentheses.

1. This shirt is both nice and cheap. (又...又...)

2. Summer in Taiwan is indeed awful! It is both hot and humid. (又... 又...)

3. This shirt is not only very expensive, but also very ugly. (不但...而 且...)

4. Li You wrote a letter to her mother last week. She wrote her another letter this week. (select 又 or 再)

5. I called her yesterday, but she wasn't home. I will call her again today. (select 又 or 再)

6. He went to a movie again last night. (select 又 or 再)

7. It was very hot yesterday, but it is even hotter today. (更)

8. I didn't know how to speak Chinese before, but now I do. (了)

9. The weather is not good today. I'm not going to the park to see the red leaves. (不 ... 了)

10. She was very busy yesterday, but she is no longer busy today. (不 ... 了)

11. What a mess! It's raining again. I'm not going out any more. (糟糕)

12. Next time you had better go to Taipei in the fall. Autumn in Taiwan is very comfortable.

13. The summer here is warm, but not hot.

Writing Practice

A. Describe today's weather.

B. Give the Chinese version of the passage below.

> I work in Taipei, but both my older brother and older sister are in Shanghai. The weather in Shanghai is different from that in Taipei. The summer in Taipei is somewhat cooler than Shanghai. Although the winter in Shanghai is colder than Taipei, it is a bit more comfortable there. I'd like to go to Shanghai to see my brother and sister this fall.

LESSON 11 ▲ Transportation

第十一課 ▲ 交通

Dì shíyī kè ▲ *Jiāotōng*

Part One

DIALOGUE: GOING HOME FOR THE WINTER VACATION

I. Listening Comprehension

A. Textbook Dialogue (True/False)

Quote the key sentence from the dialogue to support your answer.

( ) 1. Li You is leaving home for school on the twenty-first.

( ) 2. Li You should reach the airport no later than 8:00 p.m.

( ) 3. Li You decided not to take a taxi because she thought it was too expensive.

( ) 4. Li You didn't know how to get to the airport by subway.

( ) 5. In order to get to the airport, Li You can take the subway first, then the bus.

( ) 6. Li You finally agreed to go to the airport in Wang Peng's car.

B. Workbook Dialogue I (True/False)

Quote the key sentence from the dialogue to support your answer.

( ) 1. The woman has decided to go home for the summer.

( ) 2. The man invites the woman to visit his home.

( ) 3. The man and the woman will drive to the man's home together.

( ) 4. Airline tickets are not expensive now.

II. Speaking Exercises

A. Answer the questions in Chinese based on the Textbook Dialogue.

1. What will Li You do for the winter vacation?

2. Has Li You made any travel plans for her winter vacation? Explain.

3. Explain how to get to the airport from the school by bus and subway.

4. Will Li You go to the airport by taxi? Why?

B. *You need to buy airplane tickets for your winter vacation. Call your travel agent and reserve a ticket for December 22. Tell your travel agent that you prefer a morning flight.*

C. *What is the best way to get to the airport from your home? Are there any other alternatives?*

III. Reading Comprehension

A. *Answer the questions about the Textbook Dialogue.*

1. 李友的飛機票是哪天的？

2. 李友坐幾點的飛機？

3. 要是李友坐地鐵或者公共汽車，怎麼走？

4. 為什麼李友說"太麻煩了"？

5. 為什麼王朋不要李友坐出租汽車？

6. 李友最後怎麼去機場？

B. *Read the following note and answer the questions. (True/False)*

小李：

　　請你明天到我家來吃晚飯，因為明天是我的生日。到我家來你可以坐四號公共汽車，也可以坐地鐵，都很方便。坐公共汽車慢，可是不用換車。坐地鐵快，但是得換車，先坐紅線，坐三站，然後換藍線，坐兩站下車就到了。希望你能來！明天見。

　　　　　　　　　　　小白

　　　　　　　　　二月十七日下午三點

Questions:

(　)1. 小李要請小白吃晚飯。

(　)2. 坐地鐵去小白家比坐公共汽車快。

( ) 3. 坐地鐵或者坐公共汽車都得換車。

( ) 4. 小白的生日是二月八號。

( ) 5. 坐地鐵去小白家一共要坐五站，還得換車。

IV. Writing & Grammar Exercises

Grammar and Usage

A. Change the following sentences so that they reflect the "topic-comment" structure.

Example: 她喜歡那件襯衫嗎？

→ 那件襯衫她很喜歡 。

1. 你復習昨天的語法了嗎？

2. 你買飛機票了嗎？

3. 你們都很喜歡喝中國茶嗎？

4. 你不習慣這兒的天氣嗎？

B. Complete the following sentences with "還是...吧."

1. 今天的天氣真不好，別出去了，_____

_____ 。(看電視)

2. 這件衣服太貴，那件雖然顏色不好，可是
  很便宜。我 ＿＿＿＿＿＿＿＿＿＿＿＿
  ＿＿＿＿＿。(買)

3.A: 我們今天晚上吃中國飯還是吃美國飯？

  B: ＿＿＿＿＿＿＿＿＿＿＿＿＿＿＿ 。

4.A: 明天又有中國電影，又有音樂會，你說
  我們去哪兒？

  B: ＿＿＿＿＿＿＿＿＿＿＿＿＿＿＿ 。

C. Write sentences using "先...再...," based on the information given below.
  Example: 下課以後，他要去圖書館。

  →他先上課， 再去圖書館。

1. 王朋八點吃早飯，九點上電腦課。

2. 坐公共汽車以前，你得坐地鐵。

3. 我十月五日去日本，十一月六日去英國。

4. 他吃晚飯以後去看電影。

5. 李友下午兩點去圖書館，四點鐘去打球。

D. Fill in the blanks with 或者 *or* 還是.

1. 他是中國人_____美國人？

2. 到你家去，坐地鐵方便 _____坐公共汽車方便？

3. 你想買紅色的，黃色的，_____綠色的？

4. 今天晚上我想在家看書 _____看電視。

5. 我想要一杯咖啡 _____一瓶可樂。

Translation

Translate the following sentences into Chinese, using the words or phrases in parentheses.

1. It is raining. You had better stay home and watch videos. (還是...吧)

2. A: Should I take the bus or the subway to go to the airport?

   B: You can go to the airport either by bus or by subway.

3. Could you give me a ride to the airport tomorrow? (開車)

4. I have seen <u>that Chinese movie</u>. (topic-comment)

5. Let's learn the pronunciation before we learn the characters. (先...再...)

6. First, you take the bus, then change to the subway. Finally you have to take a taxi. (先...再..., 最後...)

7. It's too much trouble to write him a letter. Let's call him instead. (還是)

8. You can go to the airport by subway. First, you take the green line, and then you change to the blue line.

9. We will meet at the bus stop at 6:00 p.m.

10. Do you know where to get off?

Writing Practice

Describe in detail how to get to the airport from your school.

Part Two

A LETTER: THANKING SOMEONE FOR A RIDE

I. Listening Comprehension

A. A Letter (True/False)

Quote the key sentence from the dialogue to support your answer.

( ) 1. Wang Peng gave Li You a ride to the airport.

( ) 2. Li You cannot drive.

( ) 3. There is bus service but no subway in Li You's hometown.

( ) 4. Li You was busy visiting old friends.

( ) 5. Li You felt that everybody drove too slowly.

( ) 6. Li You very much enjoyed driving on the highway.

B. Workbook Dialogue II

( ) 1. The woman knew how to get to Little Gao's home.

( ) 2. To get to Little Gao's home by subway, one must first take the red line, then change to the blue line.

( ) 3. The woman decides to go to Little Gao's home by bus.

( ) 4. There is a bus stop in front of Little Gao's house.

C. Workbook Dialogue III

( ) 1. Old Zhang doesn't know how to drive.

( ) 2. There is a highway going to the airport.

( ) 3. Old Zhang will go to the airport with the woman.

( ) 4. The woman will go to the airport by taxi.

II. Speaking Exercises

A. Answer the questions in Chinese based on A Letter: Thanking Someone for a Ride.

1. How do you express New Year greetings in Chinese?

2. Why did Li You thank Wang Peng?

3. What has Li You been doing for the past few days?

4. Is Li You a good driver? Please explain.

B. Call your friend and thank him/her for the ride to the airport. Tell him/her what you have been doing since you returned home, and wish your friend a happy New Year.

C. Explain how to get to the airport from your friend's house by referring to the picture below.

III. Reading Comprehension

A. Answer the questions about A Letter: Thanking Someone for a Ride.

1. 為什麼李友覺得不好意思？

2. 李友回家以後，每天都做什麼？

3. 為什麼李友開車很緊張？

4. 為什麼李友開車很緊張，可是還是得自己開車？

B. Read the following diary entry and answer the questions. (True/False)

李友的一篇日記

　　今天是我第一次在高速公路上開車。我開車去小王家找他去打球。高速公路上的汽車不但多，而且都開得很快。因為我很緊張，所以迷路 (mílù: to lose one's way) 了。我的車上有電話。就給小王打電話，小王告訴我怎麼走。因為我迷路了，所以很晚才到小王家。

Questions:

(　)1. 李友常常在高速公路上開車。

(　)2. 高速公路上的汽車都開得很快。

(　)3. 李友開車的時候不緊張。

(　)4. 李友可以在她的車上打電話。

(　)5. 今天的天氣很不好，所以李友迷路了。

(　)6. 因為李友迷路了，所以小王開車來幫忙。

(　)7. 李友去小王家，因為小王請她吃晚飯。

C. Read the following note and answer the questions. (True/False)

張英，你好。我是小白。我昨天才知道你這個星期六要坐飛機去中國。你告訴王朋了，可是怎麼沒告訴我呢？你別坐公共汽車去機場。坐公共汽車不但不舒服，而且很慢。你得坐五站，還要換地鐵，太麻煩了。我可以開車送你到機場去。我們走高速公路，很快就可以到機場。我開車開得很好，因為我常常在高速公路上開車。你回學校以後給我打個電話，好嗎？要是你的飛機票已經買好了，我想知道你的飛機是幾點鐘的。好，再見。

Questions:

( ) 1. Zhang Ying will go to China with Xiao Bai.

( ) 2. Wang Peng knows that Zhang Ying is going to China.

( ) 3. According to Xiao Bai, the public transportation to the airport is not convenient.

( ) 4. Xiao Bai considers himself a good driver.

( ) 5. Xiao Bai does not know Zhang Ying's flight schedule.

D. Read the following passage and answer the questions. (True/False)

小白今天開車送張英去機場。高速公路上汽車很多，而且開得都很快，小白很緊張，所以走錯了。張英的飛機是兩點半的，可是他們三點鐘才到機場。機場的人告訴張英，她只能坐明天的飛機了。小白

▼▼▼▼▼▼▼▼▼▼▼▼▼▼▼▼▼▼▼▼▼▼▼▼▼▼▼▼▼▼▼▼▼▼▼▼

很不好意思。他說："明天我再開車送你吧。"可是張英說："謝謝。你還是在家看看錄像吧。我明天可以坐出租汽車。"

Questions:

( ) 1. Xiao Bai is a very experienced driver.

( ) 2. The traffic on the highway was light, but people drove fast.

( ) 3. Xiao Bai took the wrong way because he was nervous.

( ) 4. When they arrived at the airport, the airplane had left.

( ) 5. There were later flights today, but Zhang Ying preferred to wait till tomorrow.

( ) 6. Most likely Zhang Ying will not go to the airport with Xiao Bai tomorrow.

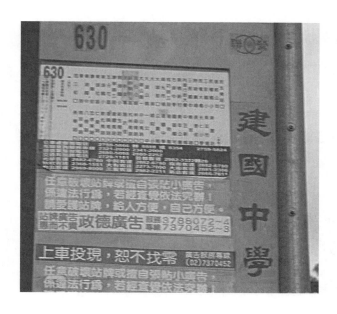

E. Read the following passage and answer the questions.

每年的中國新年小孩都很高興，因為他們不但可以穿新衣，新鞋，而且爸爸媽媽還會給他們錢。不過，小夏告訴我她不喜歡中國新年，因為她已經三十歲，有先生了。除了別人不能給她錢以外，她還得給別人錢。小夏又說新年的時候公共汽車很少，她自己也沒有車，所以出去玩也不方便。她覺得中國新年太沒意思了。

Questions:

1. What are the two things during Chinese New Year that make children so happy? Explain in detail.

2. What are the two things during Chinese New Year that make Xiao Xia unhappy? Explain in detail.

3. Is Xiao Xia male or female? How do you know?

IV. Writing & Grammar Exercises

Grammar and Usage

A. Rewrite the following sentences with 每...都 *(měi...dōu).*

Example: 他晚上看電視。

→他每天晚上都看電視。

1. 小高寫的字都很好看。

2. 她早上走高速公路。

▼▼▼▼▼▼▼▼▼▼▼▼▼▼▼▼▼▼▼▼▼▼▼▼▼▼▼▼▼▼▼▼▼▼▼▼▼

3. 考試的時候學生很緊張。

4. 小白寒假坐飛機回家。

5. 我的朋友會開車。

Translation

Translate the following sentences into Chinese, using the words or phrases in parentheses.

1. I listen to the tapes every morning. (每...都)

2. I feel really bad that I let you spend so much money.

3. For the past few days, driving on the highway every day has made me rather nervous.

4. Little Bai has no friends. So, he wished himself a Happy New Year.

▼ ▼

Writing Practice

A. *Describe your experiences driving or traveling on the highway.*

B. *Translate the following passage into Chinese.*

Winter vacation starts next week. During winter vacation I will go home to see my mom and dad. My dad bought me a plane ticket. (會) My mom called me yesterday. She told me that she had bought me three new shirts—a blue one, a red one, and a green one. Dad will drive to the airport, and my younger brother will go with him. I talked to Mom in Chinese. (用 ... V ...) She said that my Chinese had improved. I was very happy.